MOS 2013 Study Guide
for Microsoft Word Expert

John Pierce

PUBLISHED BY
Microsoft Press
A Division of Microsoft Corporation
One Microsoft Way
Redmond, Washington 98052-6399

Library of Congress Control Number: 2013941819
ISBN: 978-0-7356-6926-0

Printed and bound in the United States of America.

Third Printing: July 2015

Microsoft Press books are available through booksellers and distributors worldwide. If you need support related to this book, email Microsoft Press Book Support at mspinput@microsoft.com. Please tell us what you think of this book at http://www.microsoft.com/learning/booksurvey.

Microsoft and the trademarks listed at http://www.microsoft.com/en-us/legal/intellectualproperty/trademarks/en-us.aspx are trademarks of the Microsoft group of companies. All other marks are property of their respective owners.

The example companies, organizations, products, domain names, email addresses, logos, people, places, and events depicted herein are fictitious. No association with any real company, organization, product, domain name, email address, logo, person, place, or event is intended or should be inferred.

Acquisitions Editor: Rosemary Caperton
Editorial Production: Online Training Solutions, Inc. (OTSI)
Technical Reviewer: Rob Carr (OTSI)
Copyeditor: Kathy Krause (OTSI)
Indexer: Krista Wall (OTSI)
Cover: Microsoft Press Brand Team

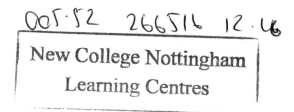

Contents

What do you think of this book? We want to hear from you!

Microsoft is interested in hearing your feedback so we can continually improve our books and learning resources for you. To participate in a brief online survey, please visit:

microsoft.com/learning/booksurvey

2   Design advanced documents   39

3   Create advanced references   77

4   Create custom Word elements   135

What do you think of this book? We want to hear from you!

Microsoft is interested in hearing your feedback so we can continually improve our books and learning resources for you. To participate in a brief online survey, please visit:

microsoft.com/learning/booksurvey

Introduction

The Microsoft Office Specialist (MOS) certification program has been designed to validate your knowledge of and ability to use programs in the Microsoft Office 2013 suite of programs, Microsoft Office 365, and Microsoft SharePoint. This book has been designed to guide you in studying the types of tasks you are likely to be required to demonstrate in Exam 77-425: Microsoft Word 2013 Expert Part One and Exam 77-426: Microsoft Word 2013 Expert Part Two.

> **See Also** For information about the tasks you are likely to be required to demonstrate in Exam 77-418: Microsoft Word 2013 Specialist, see *MOS 2013 Study Guide for Microsoft Word* by Joan Lambert (Microsoft Press, 2013).

Who this book is for

MOS 2013 Study Guide for Microsoft Word Expert is designed for experienced computer users seeking Microsoft Office Specialist Expert certification in Word 2013. This certification requires that the candidate pass two exams. This book covers the objectives of both exams.

MOS exams for individual programs are practical rather than theoretical. You must demonstrate that you can complete certain tasks or projects rather than simply answering questions about program features. The successful MOS certification candidate will have at least six months of experience using all aspects of the application on a regular basis; for example, using Word at work or school to manage and share documents, apply page layout options and styles, create reference tables and indexes, and customize Word elements such as building blocks.

As a certification candidate, you probably have a lot of experience with the program you want to become certified in. Many of the procedures described in this book will be familiar to you; others might not be. Read through each study section and ensure that you are familiar with not only the procedures included in the section, but also the concepts and tools discussed in the review information. In some cases, graphics depict the tools you will use to perform procedures related to the skill set. Study the graphics and ensure that you are familiar with all the options available for each tool.

How this book is organized

The exam coverage is divided into chapters representing broad skill sets that correlate to the functional groups covered by the exams, and each chapter is divided into sections addressing groups of related skills that correlate to the exam objectives. Each section includes review information, generic procedures, and practice tasks you can complete on your own while studying. When necessary, we provide practice files you can use to work through the practice tasks. You can practice the procedures in this book by using the practice files supplied or by using your own files. (If you use your own files, be aware that functionality in Word 2013 is limited in files saved for earlier versions of the program.)

The exam objectives are divided into four functional groups. The mapping of the exam objectives to the certification exams is shown in the following table.

Functional group	Objectives covered by Exam 77-425	Objectives covered by Exam 77-426
1 Manage and Share Documents	1.2 Prepare Documents for Review	1.1 Manage Multiple Documents 1.3 Manage Document Changes
2 Design Advanced Documents	2.1 Apply Advanced Formatting 2.2 Apply Advanced Styles	2.3 Apply Advanced Ordering and Grouping
3 Create Advanced References	3.3 Manage Forms, Fields, and Mail Merge Operations	3.1 Create and Manage Indexes 3.2 Create and Manage Reference Tables
4 Create Custom Word Elements	4.1 Create and Modify Building Blocks 4.2 Create Custom Style Sets and Templates	4.3 Prepare a Document for Internationalization and Accessibility

Candidates must pass both exams to earn the Microsoft Office Specialist Expert certification in Word 2013.

Download the practice files

Before you can complete the practice tasks in this book, you need to download the book's practice files to your computer. These practice files can be downloaded from the following page:

http://aka.ms/mosWordExp2013/files

> **Important** The Word 2013 program is not available from this website. You should purchase and install that program before using this book.

If you would like to be able to refer to the completed versions of practice files at a later time, you can save the practice files that you modify while working through the practice tasks in this book. If you save your changes and later want to repeat the task, you can download the original practice files again.

The following table lists the practice files for this book.

Folder and chapter	Files
MOSWordExpert2013\Objective1 1 Manage and share documents	*WordExpert_1-1a.docx* *WordExpert_1-1b.docx* *WordExpert_1-1c.dotx* *WordExpert_1-1d.dotx* *WordExpert_1-1e.xlsx* *WordExpert_1-2.docx* *WordExpert_1-3a.docx* *WordExpert_1-3b.docx*
MOSWordExpert2013\Objective2 2 Design advanced documents	*WordExpert_2-1.docx* *WordExpert_2-2.docx* *WordExpert_2-3a.docx* *WordExpert_2-3b.docx* *WordExpert_2-3c.docx* *WordExpert_2-3d.docx* *WordExpert_2-3e.docx*
MOSWordExpert2013\Objective3 3 Create advanced references	*WordExpert_3-1a.docx* *WordExpert_3-1b.docx* *WordExpert_3-2a.docx* *WordExpert_3-2b.docx* *WordExpert_3-2c.docx* *WordExpert_3-2d.docx* *WordExpert_3-3a.docx* *WordExpert_3-3b.xlsx* *WordExpert_3-3c.docx* *WordExpert_3-3d.docx*
MOSWordExpert2013\Objective4 4 Create custom Word elements	*WordExpert_4-1.docx* *WordExpert_4-2.docx* *WordExpert_4-3a.docx* *WordExpert_4-3b.docx* *WordExpert_4-3c.docx*

Adapting exercise steps

The screen images shown in this book were captured at a screen resolution of 1024 × 768, at 100 percent magnification. If your settings are different, the ribbon on your screen might not look the same as the one shown in this book. For example, you might have more or fewer buttons in each of the groups, the buttons you have might be represented by larger or smaller icons than those shown, or the group might be represented by a button that you click to display the group's commands. As a result, exercise instructions that involve the ribbon might require a little adaptation. Our instructions use this format:

→ On the **Insert** tab, in the **Illustrations** group, click the **Chart** button.

If the command is in a list or on a menu, our instructions use this format:

→ On the **Home** tab, in the **Editing** group, click the **Find** arrow and then, on the **Find** menu, click **Advanced Find**.

> **Tip** On subsequent instances of instructions located on the same tab or in the same group, the instructions are simplified to reflect that we've already established the working location.

If differences between your display settings and ours cause a button to appear differently on your screen than it does in this book, you can easily adapt the steps to locate the command. First click the specified tab, and then locate the specified group. If a group has been collapsed into a group list or under a group button, click the list or button to display the group's commands. If you can't immediately identify the button you want, point to likely candidates to display their names in ScreenTips.

If you prefer not to have to adapt the steps, set up your screen to match ours while you read and work through the exercises in this book.

In this book, we provide instructions based on the traditional keyboard and mouse input methods. If you're using the program on a touch-enabled device, you might be giving commands by tapping with a stylus or your finger. If so, substitute a tapping action any time we instruct you to click a user interface element. Also note that when we tell you to enter information, you can do so by typing on a keyboard, tapping an on-screen keyboard, or even speaking aloud, depending on your computer setup and your personal preferences.

Get support and give feedback

The following sections provide information about getting help with this book and contacting us to provide feedback or report errors.

Errata

We've made every effort to ensure the accuracy of this book and its companion content. Any errors that have been reported since this book was published are listed on our Microsoft Press site, which you can find at:

http://aka.ms/mosWordExp2013/errata

If you find an error that is not already listed, you can report it to us through the same page.

If you need additional support, email Microsoft Press Book Support at:

mspinput@microsoft.com

Please note that product support for Microsoft software is not offered through the preceding addresses.

We want to hear from you

At Microsoft Press, your satisfaction is our top priority, and your feedback our most valuable asset. Please tell us what you think of this book at:

http://www.microsoft.com/learning/booksurvey

The survey is short, and we read every one of your comments and ideas. Thanks in advance for your input!

Stay in touch

Let's keep the conversation going! We're on Twitter at:

http://twitter.com/MicrosoftPress

Taking a Microsoft Office Specialist exam

Desktop computing proficiency is increasingly important in today's business world. When screening, hiring, and training employees, employers can feel reassured by relying on the objectivity and consistency of technology certification to ensure the competence of their workforce. As an employee or job seeker, you can use technology certification to prove that you already have the skills you need to succeed, saving current and future employers the time and expense of training you.

Microsoft Office Specialist certification

Microsoft Office Specialist certification is designed to assist employees in validating their skills with Office programs. The following certification paths are available:

- A Microsoft Office Specialist (MOS) is an individual who has demonstrated proficiency by passing a certification exam in one or more Office programs, including Microsoft Word, Excel, PowerPoint, Outlook, Access, OneNote, or SharePoint.

- A Microsoft Office Specialist Expert (MOS Expert) is an individual who has demonstrated that he or she has mastered the more advanced features of Word or Excel by passing the required certification exams.

Selecting a certification path

When deciding which certifications you would like to pursue, you should assess the following:

- The program and program version or versions with which you are familiar
- The length of time you have used the program and how frequently you use it
- Whether you have had formal or informal training in the use of that program
- Whether you use most or all of the available program features
- Whether you are considered a go-to resource by business associates, friends, and family members who have difficulty with the program

Candidates for MOS-level certification are expected to successfully complete a wide range of standard business tasks, such as formatting a document or worksheet and its content; creating and formatting visual content; or working with SharePoint lists, libraries, Web Parts, and dashboards. Successful candidates generally have six or more months of experience with the specific Office program, including either formal, instructor-led training or self-study using MOS-approved books, guides, or interactive computer-based materials.

Candidates for MOS Expert–level certification are expected to successfully complete more complex tasks that involve using the advanced functionality of the program. Successful candidates generally have at least six months, and may have several years, of experience with the programs, including formal, instructor-led training or self-study using MOS-approved materials.

Test-taking tips

Every MOS certification exam is developed from a set of exam skill standards (referred to as the objective domain) that are derived from studies of how the Office programs are used in the workplace. Because these skill standards dictate the scope of each exam, they provide critical information about how to prepare for certification. This book follows the structure of the full objective domain for Word Expert certification; see "How this book is organized" in the Introduction for more information.

The MOS certification exams are performance based and require you to complete business-related tasks or projects in the program for which you are seeking certification. For example, you might be presented with a file and told to do something specific with it, or presented with a sample document and told to create it by using resources provided for that purpose. Your score on the exam reflects how well you perform the requested tasks or complete the project within the allotted time.

Here is some helpful information about taking the exam:

- Keep track of the time. Your exam time does not officially begin until after you finish reading the instructions provided at the beginning of the exam. During the exam, the amount of time remaining is shown at the bottom of the exam interface. You can't pause the exam after you start it.

- Pace yourself. At the beginning of the exam, you will receive information about the questions or projects that are included in the exam. Some questions will require that you complete more than one task. Each project will require that you complete multiple tasks. During the exam, the amount of time remaining to complete the questions or project, and the number of completed and remaining questions if applicable, is shown at the bottom of the exam interface.

- Read the exam instructions carefully before beginning. Follow all the instructions provided completely and accurately.

- Enter requested information as it appears in the instructions, but without duplicating the formatting unless you are specifically instructed to do so. For example, the text and values you are asked to enter might appear in the instructions in bold and underlined text, but you should enter the information without applying these formats.

- Close all dialog boxes before proceeding to the next exam question unless you are specifically instructed not to do so.

- Don't close task panes before proceeding to the next exam question unless you are specifically instructed to do so.

- If you are asked to print a document, worksheet, chart, report, or slide, perform the task, but be aware that nothing will actually be printed.

- When performing tasks to complete a project-based exam, save your work frequently.

- Don't worry about extra keystrokes or mouse clicks. Your work is scored based on its result, not on the method you use to achieve that result (unless a specific method is indicated in the instructions).

- If a computer problem occurs during the exam (for example, if the exam does not respond or the mouse no longer functions) or if a power outage occurs, contact a testing center administrator immediately. The administrator will restart the computer and return the exam to the point where the interruption occurred, with your score intact.

> **Strategy** This book includes special tips for effectively studying for the Microsoft Office Specialist exams in Strategy paragraphs such as this one.

Certification benefits

At the conclusion of the exam, you will receive a score report, indicating whether you passed the exam. If your score meets or exceeds the passing standard (the minimum required score), you will be contacted by email by the Microsoft Certification Program team. The email message you receive will include your Microsoft Certification ID and links to online resources, including the Microsoft Certified Professional site. On this site, you can download or order a printed certificate, create a virtual business card, order an ID card, view and share your certification transcript, access the Logo Builder, and access other useful and interesting resources, including special offers from Microsoft and affiliated companies.

Depending on the level of certification you achieve, you will qualify to display one of three logos on your business card and other personal promotional materials. These logos attest to the fact that you are proficient in the applications or cross-application skills necessary to achieve the certification.

Microsoft
Office Specialist

Microsoft
Office Specialist Expert

Microsoft
Office Specialist Master

Using the Logo Builder, you can create a personalized certification logo that includes the MOS logo and the specific programs in which you have achieved certification. If you achieve MOS certification in multiple programs, you can include multiple certifications in one logo.

For more information

To learn more about the Microsoft Office Specialist exams and related courseware, visit:

http://www.microsoft.com/learning/en/us/mos-certification.aspx

Exams 77-425 and 77-426

Microsoft Word 2013 Expert

This book covers the skills you need to have for certification as a Microsoft Office Specialist Expert in Microsoft Word 2013. Specifically, you need to be able to complete tasks that demonstrate the following skill sets:

1 Manage and share documents

2 Design advanced documents

3 Create advanced references

4 Create custom Word elements

With these skills, you can create, manage, and distribute documents for a variety of specialized purposes and situations. You can also customize your Word environment to enhance the productivity you need to work with advanced documents used in a business environment.

Prerequisites

We assume that you have been working with Word 2013 for at least six months and that you know how to carry out fundamental tasks that are not specifically mentioned in the objectives for these Microsoft Office Specialist Expert exams.

The certification exams and the content of this book address the processes of sharing, managing, designing, and customizing Word documents and features. We assume that you are familiar with the Office ribbon and that you understand basic Word features. This level of proficiency includes familiarity with features and tasks such as the following:

- Creating blank documents and creating documents based on templates
- Navigating through a document, including searching for text, inserting hyperlinks, and using the Go To command to find specific objects and references
- Formatting a document and text, including changing document themes, inserting simple headers and footers, and changing font attributes
- Changing document views
- Customizing the Quick Access Toolbar and the ribbon
- Printing documents, including printing document sections
- Saving documents in alternate file formats
- Working with tables and lists, including using Quick Tables, applying styles to tables, and sorting table data
- Creating simple references such as footnotes and endnotes
- Inserting and formatting objects such as shapes, SmartArt, and pictures

> **See Also** For information about the prerequisite tasks, see *MOS 2013 Study Guide for Microsoft Word* by Joan Lambert (Microsoft Press, 2013).

1 Manage and share documents

The skills tested in this section of the Microsoft Office Specialist Expert exams for Microsoft Word 2013 relate to managing and sharing documents. Specifically, the following objectives are associated with this set of skills:

1.1 Manage multiple documents

1.2 Prepare documents for review

1.3 Manage document changes

In today's work environment, you often collaborate with co-workers and colleagues to write, revise, and finalize documents. Sharing documents within a group of users often entails specific requirements and tasks. You might need to track changes that reviewers make to a document, for example, or you might need to merge copies of a document that reviewers revised independently. In some cases, documents require the protection that a password provides so that only people with the password can open and modify the file. In preparing a document in a collaborative process, you might need to restrict who can edit specific sections of the document.

This chapter guides you in studying ways to manage and share documents in Word. It covers options for tracking changes and protecting a document. It also explains aspects of working with multiple documents, such as how to copy styles and macros between templates and documents and how to organize styles.

> **Practice Files** To complete the practice tasks in this chapter, you need the practice files contained in the MOSWordExpert2013\Objective1 practice file folder. For more information, see "Download the practice files" in this book's Introduction.

1.1 Manage multiple documents

This section describes a range of features that facilitate the management of multiple documents. It describes how to merge documents, copy macros and styles, move building blocks, and link to external data from a document. It also describes how to manage different versions of a document and the different ways you can organize styles.

> **See Also** For information about creating and applying custom styles, see section 2.2, "Apply advanced styles."

Modifying existing templates

One purpose of a template is to give related documents a common look and feel. Templates provide style definitions, for example, and can contain elements such as cover pages, custom headers and footers, themes, and macros. The components of a template help you create a document to specification without needing to design the document from scratch.

If you need to modify a template that you downloaded from the Start screen or the New page of the Backstage view—or a Word template you created yourself—open the template file. Templates you create are stored by default in the Custom Office Templates folder, which is a subfolder in your Documents folder. (Word opens the Custom Office Templates folder automatically when you select Word Template in the Save As dialog box.) Templates you download from the Backstage view are saved in the AppData folder in your user profile. You can open this folder from File Explorer by entering %UserProfile%\AppData\Roaming\Microsoft\Templates in the address bar in File Explorer.

> **Tip** In Windows 8, File Explorer has replaced Windows Explorer. Throughout this book, we refer to this utility by its Windows 8 name. If your computer is running Windows 7, use Windows Explorer instead.

After you open the template, you can modify it by creating styles, changing the properties of the built-in template styles, designing a custom header or footer, inserting graphics or logos, and making similar types of changes.

Adding text and other content to a document and applying formatting to the document doesn't affect the template attached to the document. If you modify a style in a document, however, you can either apply the change only to the current document or apply the change to the template. To update the template, select New Documents Based On This Template in the Modify Style dialog box.

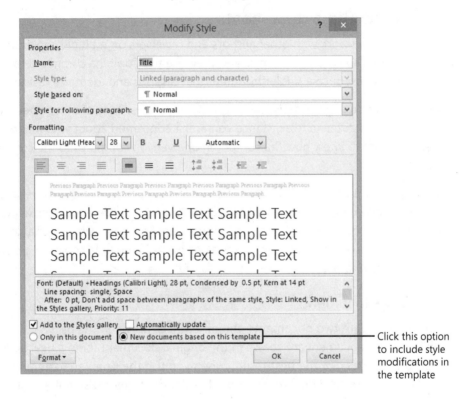

Click this option to include style modifications in the template

➤ **To modify an existing template**

1. Click the **File** tab, and then click **Open**.

2. On the **Open** page, click **Computer**, click **My Documents**, and then open the **Custom Office Templates** folder.

3. Select the template you want to modify, and then click **Open**.

4. Make the changes you want to the template's styles and other elements.

5. Click the **File** tab, and then click **Save**.

   Or

   Click the **File** tab, and then click **Save As** to save a new version of the template file.

> **Important** If you include macros in a template, you need to save the template as a Word macro-enabled template (.dotm). Save templates without macros by using the .dotx file name extension.

Merging multiple documents

In cases when you work with other authors and reviewers on multiple copies of the same document, you can collect the copies and then use the Combine command to merge the documents and produce a single document that displays and identifies revisions.

In other cases, you might simply want to compare two versions of a document to view how the versions differ. In this instance you aren't concerned about who made revisions; you simply want to know how the content in one version compares to the content in the other.

The Compare and Combine commands on the Review tab provide similar results when you merge documents, but you apply these commands in different circumstances. Use Compare when you want to view the differences between two versions of a document. Use the Combine command to merge revisions made in multiple copies of a document and to identify who made the revisions.

Comparing documents

When you compare two documents, the differences between the original document and the revised document are shown in the original document (or in a new document) as tracked changes. For the best results when you use the Compare command, the original and the revised documents should not contain any revision marks. If either document does, Word treats the changes as accepted changes when it compares the document.

In the Compare Documents dialog box, you select the original document and the revised document, choose settings for the types of changes Word will mark, and specify whether Word shows the results of the comparison in the original document, the revised document, or a new document.

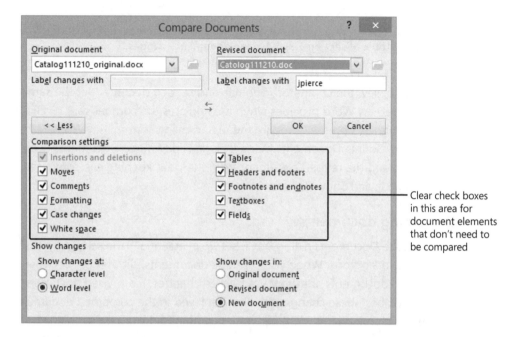

Clear check boxes in this area for document elements that don't need to be compared

By default, all the options in the Comparison Settings area are selected. You can clear the check box for any option other than Insertions And Deletions. If you don't need to view formatting differences, for example, clear the Formatting option. If you are interested chiefly in comparing the differences in the main body of each document, you might also clear the check boxes for Comments, Case Changes (whether a character is lowercase or uppercase), White Space, Headers And Footers, and Fields. In the Show Changes area, Word Level is selected by default. Select the Character Level option to show when a change is made to a few characters of a word, such as when only the case of the first let-ter is changed. At the word level, the entire word is shown as a revision; at the character level, only the letter is shown as a revision.

In the Show Changes In area, select Original Document to display the differences in that document (although you might not want to alter the original document in that way). Select Revised Document to add changes to that document, or select New Document to create a document based on the original with the differences made to the revised docu-ment shown with tracked changes.

Differences in the document created by a comparison are attributed to a single author and are displayed in a document window with the title Compared Document. You can use the Previous and Next buttons in the Review tab's Changes group to move from change to change, view the changes, and accept or reject the differences.

> **See Also** For information about accepting and rejecting changes, see the "Tracking changes" topic of section 1.3, "Manage document changes."

You can also view the compared, original, and revised document at the same time (if that isn't the view Word provides when it completes the comparison) by clicking Show Source Documents on the Compare menu and then clicking Show Both. Other options on the Show Source Documents menu include Hide Source Documents (which removes the original and the revised document from the view, keeping the compared document), Show Original, and Show Revised.

Combining documents

The Combine Documents dialog box is set up in essentially the same way as the Compare Documents dialog box. When you combine documents, differences between the original and revised documents are shown as tracked changes. If a revised document includes tracked changes, these changes are also displayed in the combined document as tracked changes. Each reviewer is identified in the combined document as well.

When you click OK in the Combine Documents dialog box, Word is likely to display a message box telling you that only one set of formatting changes can be stored in the merged document. You need to choose between the changes in the original document and the revised document to continue merging the documents. Word displays the re-sults of combining the documents in a set of windows that shows the combined docu-ment in a central pane and the original and revised documents in smaller panes at the right. Word also displays the Revisions pane along the left side of the window.

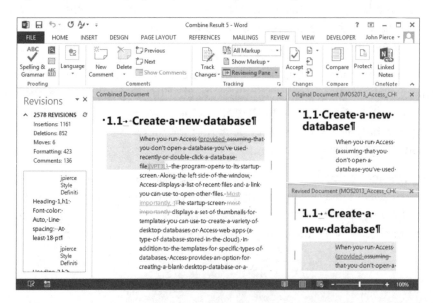

> **Tip** In the window that Word displays after you combine documents, you can scroll through the combined document and the original and revised documents at the same time. Your location in each document is synchronized, which lets you refer to any of the documents as you need to.

If you need to, you can combine another copy of the document by choosing Combine from the Compare menu again, selecting the combined result document as the original document, and selecting the next file you want to merge.

After you save and name the combined document, you can open that document and work through the variations (indicated by tracked changes), accepting and rejecting them to achieve a final document.

➤ **To compare documents**

1. Open a blank document in Word. (You can also start with the original document or the revised document open.)

2. On the **Review** tab, in the **Compare** group, click **Compare**, and then click **Compare** on the menu.

3. In the **Compare Documents** dialog box, select the original document (if it isn't already selected) from the list or by clicking the folder icon and browsing to the location where the document is saved.

4. Select the revised document you want to compare with the original document.

5. In the **Label changes with** list for the original and revised document, specify the user name or initials you want to attribute differences to.

6. If the **Comparison settings** area is not displayed, click **More**.

7. In the **Comparison settings** area, clear or select the check boxes to specify the document elements you want Word to use in its comparison.

8. In the **Show changes at** area, choose either the option to show changes at the character level or the option to show changes at the word level.

9. In the **Show changes in** area, choose an option for where you want Word to show changes: in the original document, in the revised document, or in a new document.

10. Click **OK**. If Word prompts you about tracked changes, click **Yes** to complete the comparison.

➤ **To combine two or more documents into a single document**

1. Open a blank document in Word. (You can also start with the original document or one of the revised documents open.)

2. On the **Review** tab, in the **Compare** group, click **Compare**, and then click **Combine**.

3. In the **Combine Documents** dialog box, select the original document (if it isn't already selected) from the list or by clicking the folder icon and browsing to the location where the document is saved.

4. Select the revised document you want to combine with the original document.

5. In the **Label changes with** list for the original and revised document, specify the user name or initials you want to attribute differences to.

6. If the **Comparison settings** area is not displayed, click **More**.

7. In the **Comparison settings** area, clear or select the check boxes to specify the document elements you want Word to use in its comparison.

8. In the **Show changes at** area, choose either the option to show changes at the character level or the option to show changes at the word level.

9. In the **Show changes in** area, choose an option for where you want Word to show changes: in the original document, in the revised document, or in a new document.

10. Click **OK**.

Managing versions of documents

Word uses its AutoRecover feature to save versions of a document as you write, insert content, and edit the document. The options related to automatically saving and recovering files are set on the Save page of the Word Options dialog box.

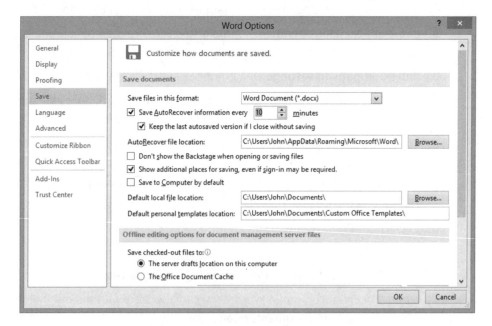

On the Save page, you can change the time interval for saving versions of your documents (the default interval is 10 minutes). You can also change the default AutoRecover file location, moving it from the AppData folder in your user profile to a folder that's more easily accessible, for example. By default, Word also retains the last version that it saved automatically if you close a document without saving it. (These settings apply only to Word and not to other Office programs.)

You can manage and recover versions of documents on the Info page of the Backstage view. Versions of the file that were saved automatically are listed in the Versions area. Right-click an item in the list to display options you can use to open that version, delete the version, or compare that version with the current one.

Word displays the Message Bar when you open an autosaved version. On the Message Bar, click Compare to view the differences between the version you opened and the last saved version. Click Restore to overwrite the last saved version with the version of the document you opened.

You can also recover an unsaved version of a document from the Info page. The Recover Unsaved Documents option displays the Open dialog box and shows the contents of the Unsaved Files folder, which is part of the AppData folder structure in your user profile. When you open the file, Word displays the Save As button on the Message Bar.

➤ **To restore an autosaved version of a document**

1. Open the file you were working on.

2. Click the **File** tab.

3. On the **Info** page, in the **Versions** area, right-click an autosaved version of the file, and then click **Open Version**.

4. In the **Message Bar**, click **Restore**, and then click **OK** to confirm the operation.

➤ **To recover an unsaved file**

1. Click the **File** tab.

2. On the **Info** page, click **Manage Versions**, and then click **Recover Unsaved Documents**.

3. In the **Open** dialog box, select the file, and then click **Open**.

4. On the **Message Bar**, click **Save As**, and then use the **Save As** dialog box to name and save the file.

Organizing styles

Specifying which styles are displayed in the Styles gallery or how Word arranges styles in the Styles pane are two of the ways you can organize styles. This section describes options for showing styles in the Styles pane and the Styles gallery, as well as how to manage styles, including how to specify a set of recommended styles. Specifying a set of recommended styles for a template helps ensure that documents based on the template retain a common look and feel.

In the Style Pane Options dialog box, you can select an option for the group of styles Word displays in the Styles pane. You can display only the set of recommended styles, the styles currently in use, the styles available in the document, or all styles. You can also select a setting for how the list of styles is sorted. For example, you can list the styles alphabetically, by type (character styles appear before paragraph styles), by font, or by ranking within the list of recommended styles. (By default, the Styles pane shows recommended styles and sorts them as recommended.)

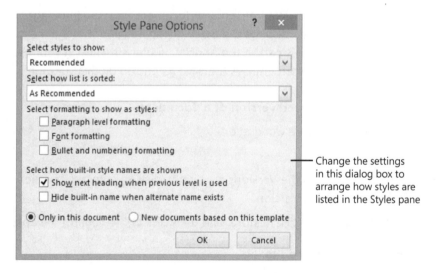

Change the settings in this dialog box to arrange how styles are listed in the Styles pane

The check boxes in the Select Formatting To Show As Styles area determine whether paragraph, font, and list formats appear in the Styles pane. For example, if you select Font Formatting, the Styles pane displays entries for the font colors used in the document. The Show Next Heading When Previous Level Is Used check box is selected by default. This setting specifies that Word will include entries for subheadings in the Styles pane when the heading above that level is used—for example, if you use the Heading 2 style in a document, Word shows the Heading 3 style in the Styles pane. Click New Documents

Based On This Template if you want to apply the settings you specify in the Style Pane Options dialog box to other documents you create with the current template.

The Manage Styles dialog box, which you can open by clicking the Manage Styles icon at the bottom of the Styles pane, provides additional settings and options for organizing styles, which it displays on the following four pages:

- **Edit** Use the options on the Edit page to view and modify the attributes of a style. Click New Style to open the Create New Style From Formatting dialog box.

> **See Also** For information about creating styles, see section 2.2, "Apply advanced styles."

- **Recommend** On the Recommend page, you can specify the set of recommended styles for a document or template. Press Ctrl and click to select a set of styles (or use the options to select all styles or all of the built-in styles). You can establish a priority for the styles in the recommended list by moving the styles up or down or by assigning a value to a style or a group of selected styles.

- **Restrict** Use the options on the Restrict page to define the set of styles a user can apply to a document when the document is protected from formatting changes.

> **See Also** For information about formatting restrictions, see the "Restricting editing" topic in section 1.2, "Prepare documents for review."

- **Set Defaults** Specify font, paragraph position, and paragraph spacing options on the Set Defaults page to define the default properties for new styles.

➤ **To arrange styles in the Styles pane**

1. On the **Home** tab, in the **Styles** group, click the dialog box launcher in the lower-right corner.

2. At the bottom of the **Styles** pane, click **Options**.

3. In the **Style Pane Options** dialog box, do any of the following:
   - ○ Select options for which styles to show and how styles are sorted.
   - ○ Specify whether to display paragraph, font, and list formatting.
   - ○ Specify how you want Word to display built-in style names.

Copying styles from template to template

By copying styles from one template to another, you can reuse styles and cut down on the work required to define styles in each template you need. If you need to copy specific styles from one template to another, you can use the Organizer dialog box.

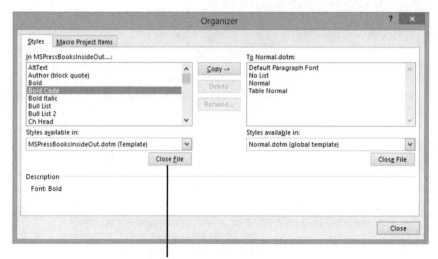

To work with the styles in a different template, click Close File. The button's label changes to Open File. Click again to locate the file you need.

The Organizer lists the styles defined in the templates (or documents) that you open by using the Organizer's list boxes. The attributes of a style you select in either list box are displayed in the Description area. Use the description to determine whether you need a style in the template to which you are copying a style. In addition to copying styles from template to template, you can delete and rename styles in the Organizer.

➤ **To copy styles between templates**

1. On the **Home** tab, in the **Styles** group, click the dialog box launcher.

2. At the bottom of the **Styles** pane, click **Manage Styles**.

3. In the **Manage Styles** dialog box, click **Import/Export**.

4. In the **Organizer**, click **Close File** and **Open File** to display the templates you want to copy styles from and to.

5. In the list box for the template you are copying styles from, select a style or styles, and then click **Copy**.

6. In the **Organizer**, click **Close**.

Copying macros from document to document

You can also use the Organizer to copy macros between documents and templates. In the Organizer, use the list boxes on the Macro Project Items page to open the template or document that contains the macros you want to copy and the template or document you want to copy the macros to.

➤ **To copy macros between documents**

1. On the **View** tab, click **Macros**, and then click **View Macros**.

2. In the **Macros** dialog box, click **Organizer**.

3. In the **Organizer**, click **Close File** and **Open File** to display the templates or documents you want to copy macros from and to.

4. In the list box for the template you are copying macros from, select the macros, and then click **Copy**.

5. In the **Organizer**, click **Close**.

Linking to external data

The topic of managing multiple documents can encompass not only working with multiple Word documents but also working with external data or files that you link to from a Word document you are working on. You can link to files created in other Office programs, in Windows-based programs such as WordPad or Paint, and Adobe Acrobat documents, for example. You can display the full contents of a file or display the file as an icon. You can also create an object (such as a chart or a slide) to insert in a Word document.

To link to external data, you use the Object dialog box. In the dialog box, you can create a new object by selecting the object type from the list on the Create New page. Select Display As Icon if you want to display an icon instead of the full object. In the Word document, you can double-click the icon to open the object.

Use the Create From File page in the Object dialog box to locate a file you want to link to. By default, Word embeds the content of the file you select in the document. Select Link To File to create a link to the source file so that updates to the source file are reflected in Word.

When you link to a file, Word displays a shortcut to the file in the Word document. Double-click this shortcut to open the source program.

➤ **To link to external data**

1. On the **Insert** tab, in the **Text** group, click **Object**.

2. In the **Object** dialog box, click the **Create from File** tab.

3. In the **File name** box, enter the name of the file you want to link to, or click **Browse** to locate the file.

4. In the **Object** dialog box, select **Link to file**.

5. Click **OK**.

Moving building blocks between documents

By default, built-in building blocks are stored in a template named Building Blocks.dotx. Word stores this file in your user profile, at the path AppData\Roaming\Microsoft\ Document Building Blocks\1033\15. (The folder named 15 stores files related to Office 2013.) You can save building blocks in templates that you design by selecting that template when you create and save a building block.

> **See Also** For more information, see section 4.1, "Create and modify building blocks."

To move a building block to a different template, which makes the building block available in documents based on that template, you use the Building Blocks Organizer. The Building Blocks Organizer lists building blocks by name, gallery, category, and template. Click the column headings to sort the list so that you can find the building block you need more easily.

➤ **To move a building block**

1. On the **Insert** tab, click **Quick Parts**, and then click **Building Blocks Organizer**.

2. In the **Building Blocks Organizer**, select the entry for the building block you want to move, and then click **Edit Properties**.

3. In the **Modify Building Block** dialog box, in the **Save in** list, select the template where you want to store the building block.

4. Click **OK** in the **Modify Building Block** dialog box, and then click **Yes** to confirm the operation.

5. Click **Close** in the **Building Blocks Organizer**.

Practice tasks

The practice files for these tasks are located in the MOSWordExpert2013\
Objective1 practice file folder. Save the results of the tasks in the same folder.

- Open Word, and then use the Combine command to merge the
  WordExpert_1-1a and *WordExpert_1-1b* documents.

- Use the Organizer to copy the style Practice Tasks from the *WordExpert_1-1c*
  template to the *WordExpert_1-1d* template.

- Create a new document based on the *WordExpert_1-1c* template (right-click
  the file, and then click New), and then modify the template by changing the
  properties for the Practice Tasks style.

- Open the *WordExpert_1-1a* document, and then use the Object dialog box to
  link to the *WordExpert_1-1e* workbook.

1.2 Prepare documents for review

Preparing a document for review often involves several steps. You can set options for
how Word tracks changes and displays revisions. You might need to restrict the editing
of a document so that reviewers can only enter comments, for example. You can also
specify sections of a document that can be edited only by certain individuals. If you plan
to distribute a document to reviewers outside your organization, you should inspect the
document to determine whether it contains information you want to remove before you
share it.

This section guides you in studying these and other steps involved in preparing documents for review.

Setting tracking options

Tracking revisions that you and other users make to a document can be simple and
straightforward. Click Track Changes on the Review tab, and then Word tracks the insertions, deletions, text moves, and formatting changes you make to the document. When
you review the revised document, you can use commands in the Changes group on the
Review tab to locate revisions and then accept or reject them.

Word provides a set of options for how the program tracks and displays revisions and how you view them. In the Track Changes Options dialog box, use the check boxes in the Show area to specify which changes to a document you want to display as you work on the document. These options include Comments, Ink, Insertions And Deletions, Formatting, and others. You can also specify what information Word displays in balloons that appear along the side of a document when you view the document in All Markup mode. For balloons, select Revisions to view each change to a document in a balloon, Nothing to show all changes inline, or Comments And Formatting to use balloons to show those elements. If you select Comments And Formatting, Word displays insertions and deletions in line with the document's text.

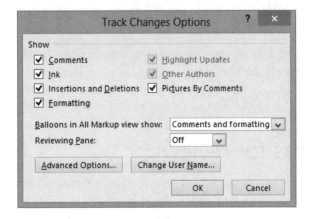

Tip Changes you make to a document are identified by the user name and initials entered in the Word Options dialog box. For some documents, you might want to be identified by your role or with a user name other than the one currently set. For example, you might want to associate revisions with the name of your department if you are reviewing a document on the department's behalf. Click Change User Name in the Track Changes Options dialog box, and then enter the user name and initials you want to use. You also need to select the option Always Use These Values Regardless Of Sign In To Office—otherwise, comments will always be identified by using the name associated with your account. Any change you make to your user name and initials or to the setting for the option Always Use These Values Regardless Of Sign In To Office is carried over to other documents and to other Office programs. You should revert to your standard user name when you want to use it.

The Advanced Options button in the Track Changes Options dialog box opens a dialog box where you can specify additional settings for how changes are tracked and displayed.

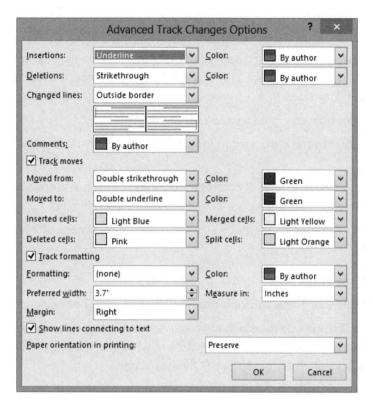

In this dialog box you can do the following:

- Select the formatting that Word applies to insertions and deletions. By default, Word underlines insertions and uses strikethrough formatting to identify deletions. Other settings include Bold, Italic, Double Underline, and Color Only.

- Specify where Word places a line that indicates where a change was made. The default setting is Outside Border. Other settings are Right Border, Left Border, and None.

- Select a color to identify your changes. By default, Word uses the By Author setting, which means that Word assigns a color to each reviewer. You can select a specific color in which to display your changes.

- Select a background color for comment balloons.

- Specify whether Word tracks text that is moved. You can select the formatting (including the color) that Word applies to the moved text in its original and new locations. If you clear the Track Moves check box, Word treats moved text as it does deletions and insertions.

- Set options for how changes to table cells are highlighted.

- Specify whether to track changes to formatting and how Word displays those changes.

- Specify the size and position of comment balloons. You can also specify whether Word shows a line that connects a balloon to the text it refers to.

- Specify how Word orients the page when you print a document with revisions and comments.

➤ **To set tracking options**

1. On the **Review** tab, in the **Tracking** group, click the dialog box launcher.

2. In the **Track Changes Options** dialog box, specify which types of changes you want Word to display as you work on the document, what information you want to view in balloons, and whether to display the **Revisions** pane.

3. Click **Advanced Options**.

4. In the **Advanced Track Changes Options** dialog box, specify the formatting settings you want Word to apply to changes tracked in the document, including insertions and deletions, text moves, and comment balloons.

Restricting editing

Only in rare cases are you likely to want to share a document and let any other user work with it at will by changing the formatting, adding or deleting content, inserting graphics, or making other modifications. Documents that contain important data or that you plan to use as the focus of a report or presentation can be protected before you share them. This section describes how to restrict the types of changes users can make to a document, specify who can edit a document, and mark which sections of a document specific individuals can edit.

> **See Also** For more information about protecting a document, see the "Protecting documents by using passwords" topic later in this section.

To control how a document can be edited, you set options in the Restrict Editing pane.

Use this area to allow specific people to edit the document or sections of a document. You can also specify sections that everyone can edit.

The pane is organized into three sections:

- **Formatting restrictions** Select the check box in this area to limit formatting to a specific set of styles and to prevent users of a document from modifying styles and applying local formatting. From the Restrict Editing pane, you can open the Formatting Restrictions dialog box, where you can specify the set of styles that is available to users working with the document. You can allow all styles, or a set of styles designated by Word, or you can select the specific styles you want to use. The options at the bottom of the Formatting Restrictions dialog box control whether users can switch themes or substitute quick styles and whether settings for automatic formatting can override the restrictions you specify.

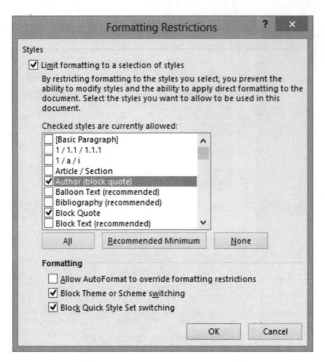

- **Editing restrictions** Use the Editing Restrictions area to control the types of changes users can make to the document.

  - **No changes (Read only)** This prevents users from making revisions, although you can set up exceptions that allow specific users to edit all or certain sections of the document.

  - **Tracked changes** Revisions made to the document are indicated by revision marks. Tracked changes cannot be turned off without removing protection from the document.

  - **Comments** Users can add comments to the document, but they can't make revisions to the document's content itself. For this option, you can set up exceptions for specific users.

    > **See also** For more information about comments, see the "Managing comments" topic in section 1.3, "Manage document changes."

  - **Filling in forms** This option lets you restrict input to filling in forms that are part of a document.

If you select No Changes (Read Only) or Comments, use the Exceptions area to specify users who can edit all or sections of a document. Exceptions apply to the complete document by default, but you can apply exceptions to a particular section of a document by selecting that section and then designating the people who can edit it. (You can also allow everyone to edit specific sections.) You can apply different exceptions to different sections of a document. Click the More Users link to open the Add Users dialog box, where you can enter the names of people who are granted the exception.

If you specify editing exceptions, you and other users can locate and display the sections of a document a specific user can edit by selecting the check box beside a user's name in the Restrict Editing pane.

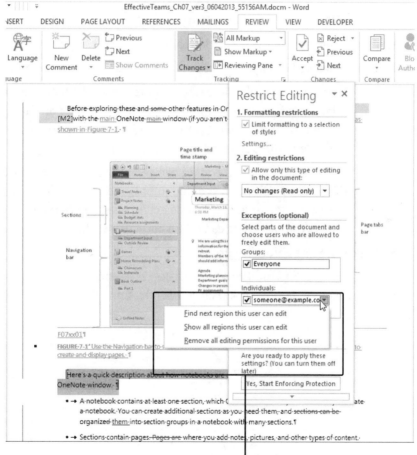

Use this menu to locate
regions that a specific user
can edit and to remove
editing permissions

- **Start Enforcement** After you define the formatting and editing restrictions you want to apply to the document, you can use the Start Enforcing Protection dialog box to define a password that's required to remove protection from the document.

> **Important** To use the User Authentication option, information rights management must be enabled for the document. Information rights management is beyond the scope of these exams. For details about information rights management, see "Configure Information Rights Management in Office 2013 at *http://technet.microsoft.com/en-us/ library/cc178985.aspx.*

➤ **To restrict editing and formatting**

1. On the **Review** tab, click **Restrict Editing**.

2. In the **Restrict Editing** pane, select the options you want to apply:

   ○ To specify a specific set of styles users can apply, click **Limit formatting to a selection of styles**, and then click **Settings**. In the **Formatting Restrictions** dialog box, select the set of styles and formatting options you want to make available in the document.

   ○ To control the type of editing allowed in the document, click **Allow only this type of editing in the document**, and then choose from the options in the list. Define exceptions by selecting a section of the document and then choosing which users can edit a particular section.

3. Click **Yes, Start Enforcing Protection**.

4. In the **Start Enforcing Protection** dialog box, enter a password that's required to remove protection or click **User Authentication**.

Deleting document draft versions

The topic "Managing versions of documents" in section 1.1, "Manage multiple documents," describes ways in which you can work with versions of a document that Word has retained. When you no longer need a specific version, you can delete it from the Info page in the Backstage view.

➤ **To delete a draft version**

   1. Click the **File** tab.

   2. On the **Info** page, in the **Versions** area, right-click the version you want to delete, and then click **Delete This Version**.

   3. Click **Yes** to confirm the operation.

Removing document metadata

Document properties (also known as metadata) identify a document by storing information such as its size, title, author, and the dates it was created and last modified. Word displays a list of standard document properties on the Info page of the Backstage view. You can display additional properties by clicking Show All Properties or by opening a document's Properties dialog box. (To open the dialog box, click the arrow beside Properties at the top of the list of properties on the Info page, and then click Advanced Properties.)

Properties provide information that you can use to classify the document, but you might not want to include this information in the version of a document you share with reviewers outside your team or organization. For example, you might want to remove the name of the document's author before sharing a document with a customer.

You can run the Document Inspector to find and remove specific types of document metadata. The Document Inspector also checks for comments and revisions still in the document, information in the header, hidden text, and other document elements. After the Document Inspector examines a document, you can choose to remove information in document properties and other areas of the document that were examined.

➤ **To inspect a document and remove document metadata**

1. Click the **File** tab.

2. On the **Info** page, click **Check for Issues**, click **Yes** if prompted to save the document, and then click **Inspect Document**.

3. In the **Document Inspector**, clear the check box for any category you don't need the Document Inspector to examine, and then click **Inspect**. The Document Inspector examines the document and displays the results.

4. In the **Document Inspector**, click **Remove All** to remove the information for a specific category.

5. Click **Close.**

   Or

   Click **Reinspect**, and then click **Inspect** to view updated results.

Marking documents as final

As a step in completing a document you have worked on with a group, you can mark the document as final so that colleagues or coworkers know the document's status. Marking a document as final does not prevent users from making changes, and it does not provide the same level of protection as applying a password to the document.

When a user opens a document that is marked final, Word displays the Message Bar, notifying the user of the document's status. The user needs to intentionally activate the document to make additional changes.

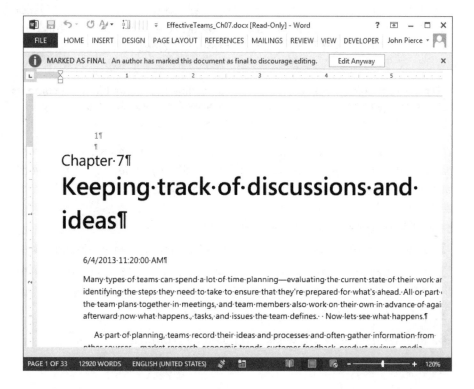

> **To mark a document as final**

1. Click the **File** tab.

2. On the **Info** page, click **Protect Document**, and then click **Mark as Final**.

3. Click **OK** to confirm the operation and save the document. (Word might display a message box describing the effects of marking a document as final. Select **Do Not Show Again** if you longer need Word to display this message, and then click **OK**.)

Protecting documents by using passwords

When you save a document by using the Save As dialog box, you can display the General Options dialog box and then define a password that users need to enter to open the document, as well as a password that's required to modify the document.

> **Important** Be careful to retain the passwords you define. Word provides no way for you to recover these passwords.

Keep in mind that requiring users to enter a password before they modify a document is intended to protect a document from unintentional editing. Defining this password does not encrypt a document to help secure it from malicious users.

> **Tip** Encryption enhances the security of a document by scrambling the contents so that it can be read only by someone who has a password or another type of key.

To protect a document through encryption, you can use the Protect Document command on the Info page of the Backstage view. When you define this password, Word cautions you that the password cannot be recovered.

➤ **To define passwords required to open or modify a document**

1. In the **Save As** dialog box, click **Tools**, and then click **General Options**.

2. In the **General Options** dialog box, enter a password for opening the document and a password for making modifications. You can define either password or both.

3. In the **General Options** dialog box, click **OK**.

4. Reenter the passwords when prompted by Word.

5. In the **Save As** dialog box, click **Save**.

➤ **To encrypt a file with a password**

1. Click the **File** tab.

2. On the **Info** page, click **Protect Document**, and then click **Encrypt with Password**.

3. In the **Encrypt Document** dialog box, enter the password you want to use, and then click **OK**.

4. Reenter the password.

5. Click **OK**, and then save the document.

Practice tasks

The practice file for these tasks is located in the MOSWordExpert2013\Objective1 practice file folder. Save the results of the tasks in the same folder.

- Open the *WordExpert_1-2* document, and do the following:
  - ○ Enable change tracking, and then insert, move, and delete some of the text. You can also add elements to the document such as images and headers or footers.
  - ○ Set different options for how Word tracks changes, and then make additional revisions to the file to view the effects of the options you selected. For example, change the formatting for insertions and deletions or clear the option to track formatting.
  - ○ Display the Restrict Editing pane. Specify settings so that only comments are permitted, but set up an exception so that you can edit the second section of the document.
  - ○ Switch to the Info page, and review the values for the document's properties. Now run the Document Inspector to remove that metadata from the file.
  - ○ Use commands in the Protect Document menu on the Info page to mark the document as final and define a password for the document.

1.3 Manage document changes

This section describes steps involved in managing document changes. It covers how to accept and reject changes, lock change tracking, and add and manage comments. It also describes options for viewing changes in a document and how to resolve style conflicts that can occur when you work with multiple documents.

Tracking changes

The Track Changes command on the Review tab turns on or off the change-tracking feature. When change tracking is enabled, Word displays insertions and deletions made to the current document's text, indicates where text was moved, and shows changes to formatting.

> **See Also** For more information, see the "Setting tracking options" topic in section 1.2, "Prepare documents for review."

You do not need to enable change tracking each time you open a document. After you turn on the feature, Word tracks changes to the document until you or another user turns the feature off. Having Word preserve the feature's status provides some assurance that important changes to a document will be recorded, but you can take an additional step to ensure that changes to a document are tracked by using the Lock Tracking option. In the Lock Tracking dialog box, you can define a password that people sharing the document must enter to turn off change tracking.

> **Important** The password you define to lock change tracking does not secure the document against malicious users. It does not encrypt the document, for example. For more information, see the "Protecting documents by using passwords" topic in section 1.2, "Prepare documents for review."

As you revise and review a document with change tracking turned on, you can use tools in the Review tab's Tracking group to change the view of a document to read it with more or less of the markup displayed. By using the Show Markup menu, for example, you can turn on or off the display of insertions and deletions, formatting changes, or comments. By selecting an option from the Display For Review list, you can view the document as though all revisions were accepted or as it was initially written.

> **See Also** For details about viewing markup and setting markup options, see the "Using markup options" and "Changing how markup is displayed" topics later in this section.

When you review a revised document, you work with the commands and options in the Changes group on the Review tab. You can move to the previous or next change and then accept or reject that change or use options on the Accept and Reject menus to act on a change and move immediately to the next change. The Accept and Reject commands also provide options that let you accept or reject only the changes shown, accept or reject all changes in the document, and accept or reject all changes and at the same time turn off change tracking.

➤ **To lock change tracking**

1. On the **Review** tab, click **Track Changes**, and then click **Lock Tracking**.
2. In the **Lock Tracking** dialog box, enter a password.
3. Enter the password a second time to confirm it, and then click **OK**.

➤ **To accept or reject a change**

1. On the **Review** tab, in the **Changes** group, click **Previous** or **Next** to locate the change.

2. In the **Changes** group, click **Accept** to incorporate the change, or click **Reject** to remove it.

➤ **To accept or reject all changes**

1. On the **Review** tab, in the **Changes** group, click the **Accept** arrow or the **Reject** arrow.

2. On the menu, click **Accept All Changes** or **Reject All Changes**.

Managing comments

Comments provide a simple way to review and annotate a document. For example, you can use comments to do the following:

- Highlight text or other content that needs to be revised or reformatted.
- Pose a question or seek clarification.
- Describe decisions to other reviewers of the document.
- Provide context or instructions for users of the document.

Word marks each comment that's inserted in a document with the name of the user who inserted it (or uses another identifying label; for example, a generic term such as Editor). When you point to a comment, Word displays information such as when the comment was inserted.

Depending on the current document view (Page Layout or Draft, for example) comments appear either in a pane along the side of a document, in the Revisions pane, or in ScreenTips. Comments are displayed in the Comments pane in the Print Layout, Read Mode, and Web Layout views. In Draft and Outline views, comments are displayed in ScreenTips when you point to the highlighted text. In any view (except Read Mode), you can open the Revisions pane to display comments. In Read Mode view, comments appear initially as comment icons. Click an icon to read the comment. Click Show Comments on the View menu in Read Mode view to display the text of a comment instead of the icon.

> **Tip** The setting you select in the Display For Review list in the Tracking group also affects how comments are displayed. For details, see the "Changing how markup is displayed" topic later in this section.

Move from one comment to the next in a document by using the Previous and Next buttons in the Comments group on the Review tab. To reply to a comment, click in a comment balloon and then click New Comment. Word identifies this comment by user name and indents it under the comment above it. Use the Delete button in the Comments group to remove a comment or to remove all comments from a file.

To manage comments, use options on the menu that Word displays when you right-click in a text in a comment balloon:

- **Reply To Comment** Inserts a comment below the original comment (or below replies entered previously). Clicking New Comment has the same effect as clicking Reply To Comment.

- **Delete Comment** Removes the comment from the document.

- **Mark Comment Done** Dims the display of the comment's text to indicate that the comment has been reviewed. In a document with numerous comments, marking comments as done helps you keep track of which comments are complete and which are active.

> **Tip** Right-clicking the thumbnail picture in a comment balloon displays a menu with different choices for managing comments and a contact card.

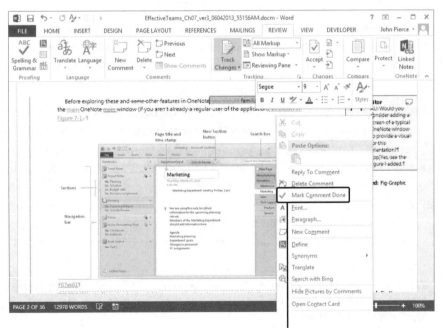

Mark a comment as done
to indicate that the comment
is resolved

If you want to emphasize the text in a comment, you can apply a limited range of font formatting from the Home tab or the Mini Toolbar. For example, you can apply bold or italic to text in a comment, highlight a comment, and change the font and font color. You cannot, however, change the size of the font.

➤ **To insert a comment**

→ On the **Review** tab, in the **Comments** group, click **New Comment**, and then enter the comment. Depending on which document view you are using, you enter the comment in a balloon or in the **Reviewing** pane.

➤ **To move from comment to comment**

→ On the Review tab, click **Next** or **Previous** in the **Comments** group.

➤ **To delete a comment**

→ Select the comment and then click **Delete** in the **Comments** group. You can also delete all comments shown or all the comments in a document.

➤ **To reply to a comment**

1. Select the comment you want to reply to.

2. On the **Review** tab, click **New Comment**, and then enter the reply.

Using markup options

When you are working in a document with change tracking turned on, you can use the Show Markup menu in the Tracking group to control the types of changes Word displays. Several of the options on the menu are the same as those provided in the Track Changes Options dialog box. For example, you can show or hide formatting changes, insertions and deletions, or comments by using the menu or the dialog box.

> **See Also** For more information about the Track Changes Options dialog box, see the "Setting tracking options" topic in section 1.2, "Prepare documents for review."

You can also use the Show Markup options to control what information Word displays in balloons in certain document views. You can show revisions in balloons or inline, or you can choose to show only formatting changes and comments in balloons.

Use the Specific People item on the Show Markup menu to view changes made by a specific reviewer or a subset of reviewers (instead of all reviewers, which is the view Word displays by default).

> **Tip** If you display changes made by a specific reviewer or a set of reviewers, use the Accept All Changes Shown and Reject All Changes Shown commands to act on that set of changes in a single step.

➤ **To turn on or off the display of markup elements**

1. On the **Review** tab, in the **Tracking** group, click **Show Markup**.

2. On the menu, clear the check mark for any markup element you want to hide.

➤ **To view changes by specific reviewers**

1. On the **Review** tab, in the **Tracking** group, click **Show Markup**.

2. On the menu, click **Specific People**, and then click **All Reviewers** to clear this setting.

3. In the **Tracking** group, click **Show Markup**, click **Specific People**, and then click the name of the reviewer whose changes you want to view. Repeat this step to view changes by additional viewers.

Resolving multidocument style conflicts

Copying and pasting text and other content is a standard operation when you work with multiple documents. If the styles in the documents you are working with have the same definitions, the text and other content will retain the formatting from the source document. If the same styles in the source and destination documents have conflicting definitions, Word uses the styles definitions in the destination document by default.

When Word detects a conflict in styles, it displays a Paste Options button. Click the button (or press Ctrl) to open a set of icons that provide options for how the content you are pasting should be formatted. You can use the destination formatting, use the source formatting, merge formatting, or keep only the text (so that the content is pasted using the default Normal style). If Live Preview is enabled, Word displays how each option affects the display of the pasted content when you point to the option's icon.

You can control how Word manages style conflicts when you paste content between multiple documents on the Advanced page of the Word Options dialog box. The settings you work with are in the Cut, Copy, And Paste section.

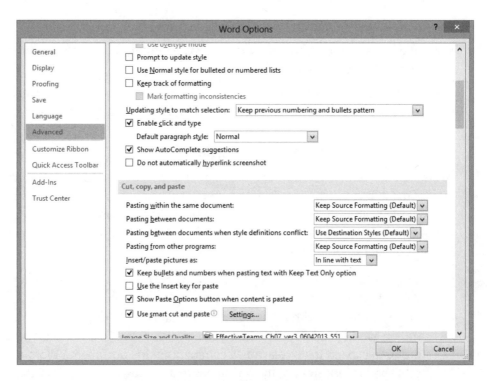

From the options in the Pasting Between Documents When Style Definitions Conflict list, select the setting that you want Word to use by default. The settings include the following:

- Use Destinations Styles (the default setting)
- Keep Source Formatting
- Merge Formatting
- Keep Text Only

In the Word Options dialog box, click the Settings button next to the Use Smart Cut And Paste option to open the Settings dialog box. The Smart Style Behavior option in this dialog box also affects how Word manages style conflicts. When this option is selected, styles are handled consistently when the style in the document you are pasting from has the same name as a style in the document you are pasting to. The Paste options allow you to choose between keeping the formatting and matching the formatting of the destination document.

➤ **To resolve style conflicts in multiple documents**

1. In the destination document, click the **Paste Options** button that Word displays when it detects a style conflict.

2. Point to the paste option icons, refer to the live preview to view how each option affects the content you are pasting, and then select the option you want to apply.

Changing how markup is displayed

Word uses the term markup to describe the set of changes tracked in a document. As part of managing the changes in a document, you can use the Display For Review list in the Review tab's Tracking group to switch between different views of the marked-up document. You can view the document as it was originally written, without any markup, or with some or all of the markup displayed.

- **Simple Markup** Word displays this view by default. With Simple Markup selected, Word displays the document as though insertions and deletions were accepted and marks a comment with a small balloon you can click to display the full comment. (When Simple Markup is selected, you can click Show Comments in the Comments group to expand the display of all comments in the document.) Word uses a vertical line to mark areas of the document that include revisions. Click that line to switch to All Markup view so that Word displays the markup.

- **All Markup** Select All Markup to display all the changes in a document, including inserted and deleted text, text moves, ink changes, and formatting changes. Word displays the marked-up document by using the settings specified in the Track Changes Options and Advanced Track Changes Options dialog boxes. For example, full comments and formatting changes are displayed in balloons if you specified that setting. In the All Markup view, you can control the types of changes Word displays and view the changes made by specific reviewers by using the Show Markup menu.

> **See Also** For details about settings on the Show Markup menu, see the "Using markup options" topic earlier in this section. For information about options for tracked changes, see the "Setting tracking options" topic in section 1.2, "Prepare documents for review."

- **No Markup** Select this option to view the document as though all changes have been accepted. Word does not display a line indicating the location of revisions.

- **Original** Select this option to view the document as it was initially written (as though all insertions, deletions, and text moves have been rejected).

➤ **To change the markup that is displayed**

→ On the **Review** tab, in the **Tracking** group, open the **Display For Review** list, and then select the option you want to use to view markup in the document.

Practice tasks

The practice files for these tasks are located in the MOSWordExpert2013\ Objective1 practice file folder. Save the results of the tasks in the same folder.

- Open the *WordExpert_1-3a* document and do the following:
  - ○ Work with the Show Markup menu and the Display For Review menu to view how these options affect the view of the document's markup.
  - ○ Insert one or more comments, and then mark the comments already in the file as complete.
  - ○ Use the options on the Review tab to move through the document and accept and reject revisions.
- Open the *WordExpert_1-3b* document. Copy text in this document, and then paste it into the *WordExpert_1-3a* document. Use the Paste Options button to resolve the style conflict.

Objective review

Before finishing this chapter, ensure that you have mastered the following skills:

1.1 Manage multiple documents
1.2 Prepare documents for review
1.3 Manage document changes

2 Design advanced documents

The skills tested in this section of the Microsoft Office Specialist Expert exams for Microsoft Word 2013 relate to designing advanced documents. Specifically, the following objectives are associated with this set of skills:

2.1 Apply advanced formatting

2.2 Apply advanced styles

2.3 Apply advanced ordering and grouping

This chapter guides you in studying the ways in which you can design, format, and organize longer, more complex documents, such as reports, books, dissertations, and requests for proposals. In particular, this chapter describes how to create and manage a document outline and how to work with master documents. It also describes how to create and modify styles so that you can more easily format a long document and keep the document's appearance consistent. To begin, this chapter explains some of the advanced formatting features in Word, including how to use wildcards to search for patterns in text, how to format fields, and how to work with features such as character spacing, kerning, page layout options, document sections, and text boxes.

> **Practice Files** To complete the practice tasks in this chapter, you need the practice files contained in the MOSWordExpert2013\Objective2 practice file folder. For more information, see "Download the practice files" in this book's Introduction.

2.1 Apply advanced formatting

This section explains how to work with features related to advanced formatting. It first describes how wildcard characters function to find text patterns in a document. It also describes custom field formats and advanced page layout options, including how to insert document sections. In addition, this section explains special character formatting that you can apply to improve the presentation of a document, such as character spacing and character sets, which provide a highly decorative appearance suitable for certificates, diplomas, and similar types of documents. The last topic in this section explains how to link text boxes, a step you might need to take when you design newsletters or other multicolumn documents.

Using wildcards in find-and-replace searches

Simple find-and-replace operations in Word can be extended in several ways. In the Find And Replace dialog box, for example, you can select an option to search only for whole words, use a case-specific search (*they're* instead of *They're*), or search by using how words sound (*they're, their,* and *there*). You can also search for text with specific formatting (for example, searching for text with the Emphasis style applied to it) and for special characters and formatting marks (including an en dash, an em dash, a paragraph mark, a tab character, and a section break).

You can also extend your use of the Find And Replace dialog box by using wildcards. For example, as a wildcard character, the asterisk (*) represents a sequence of one or more characters. The question mark (?) is used to represent a single character within a sequence. When you combine wildcard characters with literal characters, you can find patterns of text.

The following table lists wildcard characters and examples of how to use them.

Wildcard character	Syntax and examples
?	Locates any single character. For example, *l?w* locates the words *law* and *low* and this sequence of characters in words such as *below* or *lawful*.
*	Locates a string of characters. For example, *J*n* finds *John, Jocelyn,* and *Johnson*.
<	Finds characters at the start of a word. For example, *<(plen)* finds *plenty, plentiful,* and *plentitude*. It would not find the word *splendid*.
>	Finds characters at the end of the word. For example, *(ful)>* finds *fanciful, useful,* and *plentiful*. It does not find *fulfill* or *wonderfully*.

Wildcard character	Syntax and examples
[ ]	Finds one of the characters that you specify. For example, *h[eor]s* finds words such as *ghosts, these, hose, those*, and *searches*, or the abbreviation *hrs* (hours). It does not find *horse*.
[*n-n*]	Finds any single character within the range you specify. You must specify the range in ascending order (*d-l*, for example). Using *[c-h]ave*, for example, finds *gave, have*, and *leave*.
[!*n-n*]	Finds any single character except the characters in the range you specify. For example *st[!n-z]ck* finds *stack* and *stick* but not *stock* or *stuck*.
{*n*}	Finds the specified number of instances of the previous character or expression. For example, *cre{2}d* finds *creed* but does not find *credential*.
{*n,*}	Finds at least the specified number of instances of the preceding character or expression. For example, *cre{1,}d* finds both *creed* and *credential*.
{*n,m*}	Finds the number of instances of the preceding character or expression in a range. For example, *50{1,3}* finds *50, 500*, and *5000*.
@	Finds one or more instances of the preceding character or expression. For example, *bal@** finds *balloon* and *balcony*.
[*wildcard character*]	Finds instances of the specified wildcard character. For example, [*] finds all asterisk wildcard characters.

As shown in the example for the @ symbol, you can combine wildcard characters to create expressions. For example, the expression *s[a-n]{2}d* finds words such as *send, sending, dashed*, and *slide*, but does not find the word *sad*. In this expression, Word searches for a string of characters that starts with *s*, contains two characters within the range *a-n*, and ends with *d*. You can also use parentheses to group wildcard characters and text to indicate the order of evaluation. For example, the expression *<(det)*(ing)>* finds *determining* and *deterring*. Keep in mind that all searches in which you use wildcards are case-specific. For example, the expression *[c-h]ave* finds *have* and *cave* but not the name *Dave*.

> **Tip** When the Use Wildcards option is selected in the Find And Replace dialog box, the wildcard characters you can use appear on the Special menu. Select a character, or enter the character or characters you want to use in the Find What and Replace boxes.

You can use wildcards to replace patterns of text as well. For example, you can use the \n wildcard character to invert first and last names by entering (*First Name*) (*Last Name*) in the Find What box and \2 \1 in the Replace With box. Word finds occurrences of the name and inverts the order so that the last name (item 2) comes first.

➤ **To search by using wildcard characters**

1. On the **Home** tab, in the **Editing** group, click the arrow next to **Find**, and then click **Advanced Find**.

2. In the **Find and Replace** dialog box, click **More** to display the **Search Options** area.

3. Select **Use Wildcards**.

4. Enter the wildcard expression in the **Find What** box, and then click **Find Next**.

Creating custom field formats

Word uses fields to display information such as page numbers, entries in indexes and tables of contents, and figure captions. Fields are also used in mail merges to display name and address information, for example.

> **See Also** For more information about working with indexes, tables of contents, and figure captions, see section 3.1, "Create and manage indexes" and section 3.2, "Create and manage reference tables." For information about the mail merge feature, see section 3.3, "Manage forms, fields, and mail merge operations."

You can format fields as you do text or other elements in a document. For example, you can apply font and paragraph formatting so that the field's information appears the same as the text surrounding it. You can also use built-in switches to instruct Word how to display the information the field provides.

> **Tip** When you select some fields—a date and time field, for example—Word shades the field in light gray to indicate that the information is derived from a field. You can control when Word displays field shading by setting an option on the Advanced page of the Word Options dialog box. In the Show Document Content area, set Field Shading to When Selected (the default setting), Always, or Never.

The Field dialog box lists fields in a variety of categories, such as Date And Time, Document Automation, Document Information, and Mail Merge. When you select a field, the Field dialog box displays the field's properties and options for how Word displays the field's information. (For example, you can choose different calendars as the basis for the Date field.) A description of the field appears at the bottom of the dialog box.

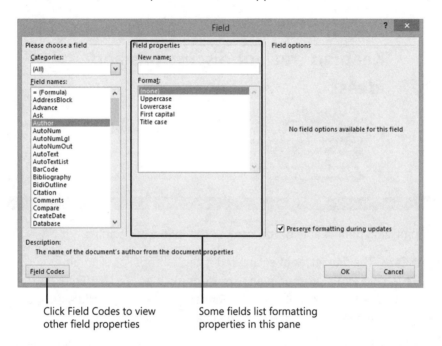

Click Field Codes to view other field properties

Some fields list formatting properties in this pane

Not all fields have properties. A field such as Author includes formatting options that display the field's value (the document's author's name) in uppercase (JOHN PIERCE), lowercase (john pierce), title case (John Pierce), or with an initial capital letter (John pierce). The Date field also has a selection of built-in formats that show the date and time in different configurations (5/09/14; May 9, 2014; May 9; May-9; and others).

The formatting of a field is controlled by the use of switches, which are a set of characters that instructs Word how to display the field. Word includes switches for the capitalization of text, numeric formats, and character formats. You can enter switches in the Field dialog box when you insert a field or within the field code in the body of the document.

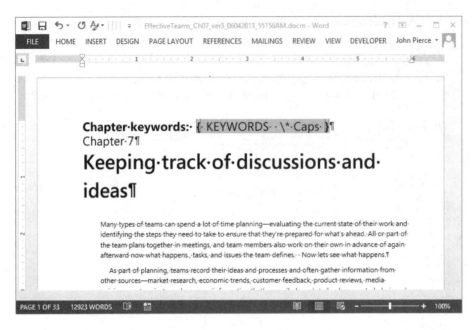

For capitalizing data in a field, you can use the following formats:

- *** Caps** The first letter of each word is capitalized. For example, you could use the Fill-In field and a prompt in an expression such as { FILLIN "Enter your name:" * Caps }. Even if a user enters his or her name in lowercase characters, the user's first and last names are formatted with initial capitals.

- *** FirstCap** The first letter of the first word is capitalized. For example, with the Comments field, an expression such as { COMMENTS * FirstCap } displays the value entered in the document's Comments field with an initial capital letter (as in *Monthly progress report*).

- *** Upper** All characters appear in uppercase. For example, { KEYWORDS * Upper } shows the keywords defined in a document in uppercase.

- *** Lower** All characters are lowercase. For example, { FILENAME * Lower } displays the document's file name in all lowercase characters.

The following list describes some of the switches you can apply to format numbers and characters in fields:

- *** Arabic** Displays the field's data as Arabic cardinal numerals. For example, { PAGE * Arabic } displays page numbers such as 11, 16, and 107. If the setting selected in the Number Format area of the Page Number Format dialog box is not Arabic, using this switch overrides the setting in the dialog box.

- *** roman** Displays the field's data as Roman numerals. The data is displayed in the same case as the word *roman* in the field code. For example, { PAGE * roman } displays vii, and { PAGE * ROMAN } displays VII.

- *** MERGEFORMAT** Maintains the formatting of the field when the field is updated. For example, if you apply italics to the keywords displayed by the field code { KEYWORDS * MERGEFORMAT }, Word retains the formatting when keywords change or are updated. When you insert fields by using the Field dialog box, Word includes the * MERGEFORMAT switch by default. Turn off this option by clearing the Preserve Formatting During Updates check box in the dialog box.

➤ **To apply formats to field data**

1. On the **Insert** tab, in the **Text** group, click **Quick Parts**, and then click **Field**.
2. In the **Field** dialog box, in the **Field Names** list, select the field you want to add to the document.
3. Click **Field Codes** to display the **Advanced Field Properties** area.
4. In the **Field Codes** box, enter the formatting switch you want to use, and then click **OK**.

➤ **To insert switches in the field code**

1. In the document, right-click the field, and then click **Toggle Field Codes**.
2. In the field code, after the field name, enter the formatting switch you want to use.
3. Right-click the field code, and then click **Update Field** to display the results.

Using advanced layout options

The layout of a Word document involves elements such as margins, page size, page orientation, and columns. Other elements of a document's layout include a header or a footer, borders, and page and section breaks. You control the layout of a Word document by applying options from the Page Layout tab and other command groups on the ribbon. For more advanced layout options, you often work in the Page Setup dialog box and in dialog boxes with settings that affect the layout of paragraphs and columns.

> **See Also** For details about inserting and working with sections, see the "Working with document sections" topic later in this section.

Setting up pages

The Page Setup group on the Page Layout tab provides built-in commands that you can use to set margins, page orientation, page size, and the number of columns—for example, narrow or wide margins, legal and other paper sizes, and two or three columns. To fine-tune the built-in settings and work with more advanced options for setting up a page, you can open the Page Setup dialog box.

On the Margins page of the dialog box, the settings in the Margins area determine the width of a document's margins along its boundaries. Increasing the value in the Gutter box (which is 0 inches by default) creates space that can be used to bind facing pages, as in a bound book or a report.

The setting in the Multiple Pages list changes options for margins and a gutter

The setting specified in the Pages area, in the Multiple Pages list, affects which margins you set.

- **Normal** Set margins for Top, Bottom, Left, and Right. You can specify the measurement for a gutter and position the gutter at the left or the top of the document. (The Preview area in the dialog box shows how settings affect the document's layout.)

- **Mirror margins** This setting applies to a document you are printing on both sides of a sheet. With this setting, you set margins for the Top, Bottom, Inside, and Outside. You can set a gutter to appear between pages (where the pages might be bound).

- **2 pages per sheet** The margin settings for this option are Outside, Inside, Left, and Right. You can also set a gutter along the top and bottom of the page.

- **Book fold** The settings for Book Fold are Top, Bottom, Inside, and Outside. You can specify a gutter between facing pages.

The Paper page of the Page Setup dialog box provides a list with the same paper sizes shown on the Size menu on the ribbon, but it also includes the Custom Size option. With this option, you can specify the width and height of the page. For example, a book might use a page size of 7 inches by 9 inches instead of the standard letter-size page. In a document in which you have defined more than one section, you can specify a different paper source (a printer tray) for each section if you need to.

> **See Also** For information about working with the Layout page of the Page Setup dialog box, see the "Working with document sections" topic later in this section.

The Page Layout tab's Page Setup group also provides options for using columns in a document's layout. The Columns dialog box provides five preset choices for columns (the same set as on the Column menu in the Page Setup group) and a list in which you can specify up to 13 columns for a page. You can adjust the column width (by default, multiple columns have an equal width) and the spacing between columns, and you can display a line between columns.

Use the Breaks menu on the ribbon to insert manual page breaks, column breaks, and section breaks. The Text Wrapping command on the Breaks menu inserts additional space to keep text and objects more distinct.

The Line Numbers command inserts line numbers along the left margin of a document. Line numbers are often used in legal documents for ease of reference. You can select an option to display line numbers continuously through a document, or to start line numbering with each new page or section. You can also set line numbering options such as the distance between line numbers and text.

Hyphenation also affects the appearance of a page. Word by default does not hyphenate a document. If you choose to have Word hyphenate a document automatically, you can set an option to limit the number of consecutive hyphens. If you hyphenate a document manually, Word displays a dialog box in which you can confirm the hyphenation Word suggests or reposition a hyphen within a word.

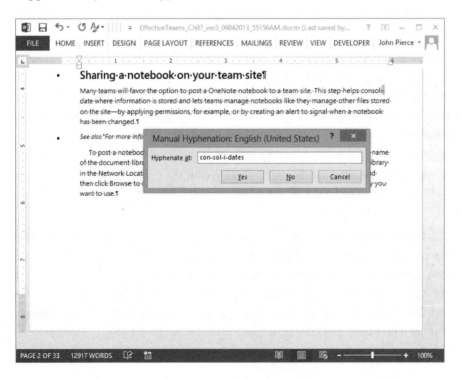

➤ **To set custom margins**

1. On the **Page Layout** tab, in the **Page Setup** group, click **Margins**, and then click **Custom Margins**.

2. On the **Margins** page of the **Page Setup** dialog box, in the **Pages** area, select the configuration you want to apply to the document: **Normal**, **Mirror margins**, **2 pages per sheet**, or **Book fold**.

3. In the **Margins** area, enter the values for margins and a gutter if the page layout requires one.

4. In the **Apply to** list, select the option for the scope of these settings: **This section**, **This point forward**, or **Whole document**.

5. Click **OK**.

➤ **To set a custom paper size**

1. On the **Page Layout** tab, in the **Page Setup** group, click **Size**, and then click **More Paper Sizes**.

2. On the **Paper** page of the **Page Setup** dialog box, in the **Paper Size** list, select **Custom Size**.

3. In the **Width** and **Height** boxes, enter the dimensions for the page size.

4. In the **Apply to** list, select the option for the scope of these settings: **This section**, **This point forward**, or **Whole document**.

5. Click **OK**.

➤ **To set up custom columns**

1. On the **Page Layout** tab, in the **Page Setup** group, click **Columns**, and then click **More Columns**.

2. In the **Columns** dialog box, select a preset number or layout of columns, or use the **Number of columns** box to specify the number of columns you want to create.

3. In the **Width and spacing** area, specify settings for the width and spacing for a column or columns, or keep **Equal column width** selected.

4. In the **Apply to** list, select the option for the scope of these settings: **This section**, **This point forward**, or **Whole document**.

5. Click **OK**.

Adjusting paragraph spacing and indentation

Use the options in the Paragraph group on the Page Layout tab to change the indentation of text and the spacing before and after paragraphs. The dialog box launcher in the Paragraph group opens the Paragraph dialog box with the Indents And Spacing page displayed.

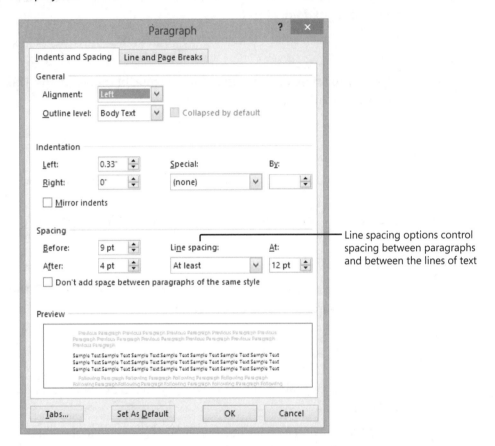

Line spacing options control spacing between paragraphs and between the lines of text

With the options in the Paragraph dialog box, you can refine indentation and line spacing settings. In the Indentation area, select Mirror Indents if you are setting up a document to print on both sides of a sheet. The Special list is used to create paragraphs in which the first line is indented more than other lines, or a hanging indent, in which the first line is indented less. A hanging indent is often used to create bulleted lists.

In the Spacing area, select a standard setting from the Line Spacing list (Single, Double, or 1.5) or use the At Least or Exactly option. With both of these options, you specify a value for line spacing in the At list. With the At Least option, Word uses either this value or the size to fit the largest font or graphic in a line. The Exactly option applies the height you specify regardless of content.

➤ **To adjust paragraph specifications**

1. On the **Page Layout** tab, in the **Paragraph** group, click the dialog box launcher.

2. In the **Paragraph** dialog box, set indentation for the left and right sides of the page.

Or

Select **Mirror indents**, and then specify values for the inside and outside borders of the page.

3. In the **Spacing** area, specify spacing for before and after a paragraph.

4. In the **Line Spacing** list, select a standard setting, or select **Exactly** or **At Least** and then specify the line spacing you want to use.

5. Click **OK**.

Arranging objects on pages

When you lay out a document that contains illustrations, images, charts, or other objects, you can use the options in the Arrange group on the Page Layout tab to position the objects and specify how text wraps around them. You can also change the order of objects and specify how objects are aligned within the document. You are likely to need to arrange objects when you are producing documents such as newsletters, magazines, and illustrated reports.

Text and objects appear on different "layers" in a document. You can position an object in line with a document's text—on the same layer—which means that the object can be positioned only within a single paragraph, with no text wrapping around the object. When you wrap text around an object, you can position an object anywhere within the document, even behind text, as you would with a watermark.

> **Tip** Use Bring Forward, Send Backward, and related commands to change the position of an object in relation to other objects and to text.

Word provides several preset position and wrapping options. Use the options in the Position gallery in the Arrange group to orient the object on the page, either in line with the text or positioned at the top, middle, or bottom along either margin, or centered within the text at the top, middle, or bottom of the page. Options on the Wrap Text menu adjust how the object and text appear together. The Tight option, for example, causes the text to wrap to reflect the object's shape and dimensions. The Square option positions text roughly equally along each side of an object.

You can drag an object to change its position or use the Layout dialog box to work with a variety of options that effect the object's position, size, and relationship to text. (Open the Layout dialog box by clicking More Layout Options at the bottom of the Position or Wrap Text menu.)

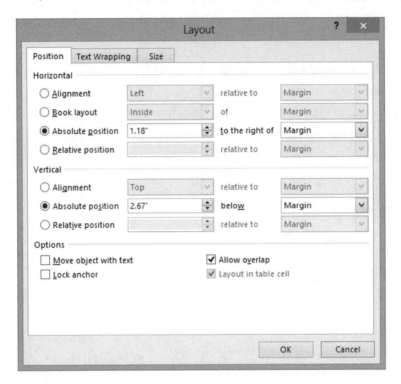

In the Layout dialog box, the options and settings in the Horizontal and Vertical areas affect the position of the object in relation to the margin, page, paragraph, or line. You can position the object at the distance you specify (Absolute Position) or use a relative position in case the document's margin changes, for example. Other options on the Position page of the Layout dialog box can be used to anchor the object on the page or allow the object to move when text is inserted or deleted.

In addition to the preset wrapping options, the Text Wrapping page provides options that you can use to specify whether text wraps on only a single side of an object or on the side with the most space (Largest Only). You can also specify values for the distance the text remains from the object along the top, bottom, and sides.

The Size page of the Layout dialog box provides settings you use to precisely control the height, width, rotation, and scale of an object.

> **Tip** The options and commands in the Arrange group on the Page Layout tab are also available on the Picture Tools Format tool tab. By switching to the Format tool tab, you can arrange objects and also have access to commands to apply styles and formatting effects such as borders and shadows.

> ➤ **To arrange an object on a page**

1. Select the object.

2. On the **Page Layout** tab, in the **Arrange** group, click **Position**, and then select an option to position the object on the page.

3. In the **Arrange** group, click **Wrap Text**, and then click the option for how you want text to wrap.

4. Click **Wrap Text**, and then click **More Layout Options**.

5. In the **Layout** dialog box, use the settings on the **Position**, **Text Wrapping**, and **Size** pages to adjust the position and alignment of the object.

Working with document sections

By creating sections within a document, you can apply different page layout options to each section. For example, in a document that includes wide tables and illustrations in addition to text, the text sections could use the default Portrait orientation, and you could create sections in which to include the tables and illustrations and then set the page orientation for those sections to Landscape. You can change the settings for the following elements within a document section:

- **Headers and footers** Text and page numbering in the headers or footers can differ between sections.

- **Footnotes** Note numbers can restart within a section (or notes can be numbered consecutively through a document).

- **Margins** Indentation can vary between sections.

- **Page orientation** One section can use Landscape orientation, and another can use the Portrait setting.

- **Paper size** One section can use letter size while another section uses legal.

- **Columns** The number of columns can vary in different document sections.

When you insert a section break, you can choose from four types:

- **Next Page** Starts the new section on the next page.

- **Continuous** Starts the new section on the same page as the current section. You can, for example, have sections with a different number of columns on the same page.

- **Even Page** Starts the new section on the next even-numbered page. (If the following page is an odd-numbered page, that page is left blank).

- **Odd Page** Starts the new section on the next odd-numbered page. (If the following is an even-numbered page, that page is left blank).

> **Tip** Word inserts section breaks automatically when you apply certain formatting to selected text. For example, if you select one or more paragraphs on a page and then format those paragraphs so that they appear in two or three columns, Word inserts continuous section breaks before and after the selected text.

The Layout page of the Page Setup dialog box contains settings related to sections. You can display the Layout page by double-clicking the marker for a section break.

The Section Start area of the Layout page shows the type of section break. With the insertion point in the section following a section break, you can use the Section Start list to change the type of section break (from Continuous to Next Page, for example). On the Layout page, you can also select an option for using different headers and footers on odd and even pages within a section and using a different header on the first page of a section. When you define a header or a footer for a section, you can use the Link To Previous command (in the Navigation group on the Header & Footer Design tool tab) to break the link between the header and footer in the previous section and create a new header or footer for the current section.

> **Important** If you delete a section break, any section formatting applied to the content or pages in that section reverts to the formatting specified for the section that follows the deleted section.

➤ **To insert a section break**

1. Click in the document where you want the new section to start.

2. On the **Page Layout** tab, in the **Page Setup** group, click **Breaks**, and then select the type of section break to insert: **Next Page**, **Continuous**, **Even Page**, or **Odd Page**.

➤ **To delete a section break**

1. Press **Ctrl+Shift+8** to display formatting marks.

2. Select the section break you want to delete, and then press **Delete**.

➤ **To change the type of section break**

1. Place the cursor in the section that follows the section break you want to change.

2. On the **Page Layout** tab, click the dialog box launcher in the **Page Setup** group.

3. In the **Page Setup** dialog box, click the **Layout** tab.

4. In the **Section start** list, select the type of section you want to apply to the preceding section break.

5. Click **OK**.

Setting character spacing options and advanced character attributes

The Advanced page of the Font dialog box provides tools for adjusting character spacing, kerning, and other typographic features. These settings and options are especially useful when you are working with display type such as headings or when you need special ornamentation in a document such as a certificate.

In the Character Spacing area, the Scale list specifies the percentage by which Word expands characters to cover a larger area or condenses them to reduce space. (The Preview area on the Advanced page shows the effect of the selection you make, as it does for other settings on this page). The Spacing list provides settings (Normal,

Expanded, or Condensed) that increase or decrease the spacing between characters. For the Expanded and Condensed settings, the By box controls the amount of space Word adds or subtracts. By default, Word uses 1 point. Similarly, the three settings in the Position list (Normal, Raised, or Lowered) affect a character's position in relation to a baseline—the amount a character is raised or lowered is controlled in the By box.

Kerning is another option for finely controlling the spacing of characters. Kerning isn't as noticeable in font sizes used in the body of a document, but in prominent headings that use a large-size font (and especially between certain sets of characters, such as an F and an L), kerning can help legibility. Word applies kerning when the Kerning For Fonts check box is selected. Word uses the setting specified in the Points And Above list to determine at which point size to start applying it.

The settings in the OpenType Features area of the Advanced page apply only to certain OpenType fonts. (OpenType fonts are related to TrueType fonts and are used on many different computer systems.) Some of these fonts—such as Calibri, Cambria, Constantia, Corbel, and Gabriola—are included in Windows and Office. The following list describes the settings in the OpenType Features area:

- **Ligatures** A ligature is a character in which two or more letters are combined. Ligatures are used for aesthetic effect. Font designers can choose whether to include ligatures in one or more of the following categories. You can choose options to use ligatures from all these categories or from none.

    - **Standard Only** Standard ligatures vary by language. In English, common ligatures join f, l, or i with a preceding f.

    - **Standard and Contextual** This setting includes character combinations designed specifically for the font.

    - **Historical and Discretionary** These ligatures included combinations (such as ct and st) that were once standard.

- **Number spacing** Fonts such as Candara, Constantia, and Corbel use proportional number spacing by default. The varying widths of the numbers make these fonts well suited for use within text. Fonts such as Calibri, Cambria, and Consolas use tabular spacing by default. Tabular numbers have the same width. These fonts are useful when you need to align columns of numbers in tables of numeric data.

- **Number forms** Numerical characters that use the "old style" vary in height and are often used when the numbers appear in text because they align easily with a mix of uppercase and lowercase characters. Lining-style numbers align on the baseline and are of equal height. They are used more for numerical data. The fonts Candara, Constantia, and Corbel use old-style numbers by default. Calibri, Cambria, and Consolas use the lining style as their default number form.

- **Stylistic sets** Some fonts (Gabriola, for one) come with highly stylized combinations of characters for use in decorative text. Use the Stylistic Sets list to select one of the available sets. You'll often want to try more than one to get the effect you want, and you can apply different sets to different characters.

> **Tip** To check whether a font uses old-style or lining numbers by default, open Fonts in Control Panel and then double-click the font. The style for numbers shown in the font's sample text is usually that font's default style. In general, fonts that use old-style numbers also use proportional spacing. Similarly, fonts that use lining-style numbers most often use tabular spacing as their default setting.
>
> If you want to check whether any ligatures are included in a font, open Character Map in Windows. (In Windows 8, enter *character map* at the Start screen.) Select the font you want to examine, scroll to the bottom of the list of characters, and then check for fl and other ligatures.

Linking text boxes

In most Word documents, text appears between defined margins and flows from page to page. In documents such as newsletters or reports, where you might want to place text in a particular location to emphasize it, you can use a text box. You can work with text boxes in ways similar to how you manage other objects (such as images or shapes) that you add to a document from the Insert tab. You can add a border or a fill to a text box, for example. You can also rotate a text box.

> **Tip** When you add a text box to a document, you can choose one of several built-in text box styles or draw a text box yourself to define the box's boundaries. You can then use the handles that appear when the text box is selected to change its dimensions and orientation.

When you add two or more text boxes to a document (for a newsletter, for example), you can link text boxes to facilitate the flow and editing of the text that the text boxes contain. When text boxes are linked, any text that does not fit within the boundaries of the first text box flows automatically into the linked text box. If you shorten or lengthen the text in linked text boxes, the text reflows to reflect the change.

> **Important** You can link only to an empty text box. Word displays an error message if you try to create a link to a text box that already contains text.

Word displays visual hints during the steps you follow to link text boxes. The mouse pointer changes during this process to resemble first an upright cup (when you select the first text box) and then a cup spilling letters, which is your clue that when you select the second text box, text will flow to it from the first.

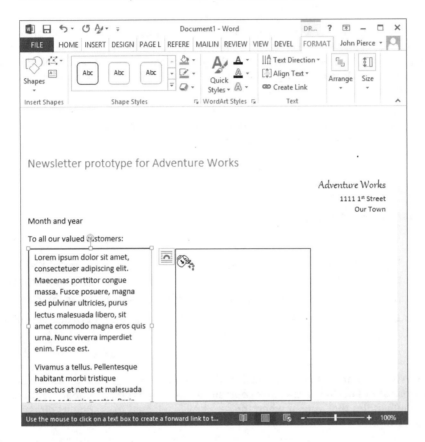

> ➤ **To link text boxes**

1. Select the text box you want to link to another text box.

2. On the **Format** tool tab, click **Create Link** in the **Text** group.

3. Move to the text box you want to link to, and then click in that text box.

➤ **To break links between text boxes**

1. Select the text box you linked to another text box (the text box you selected in step 1 in the preceding procedure).

2. On the **Format** tool tab, click **Break Link** in the **Text Group**.

Practice tasks

The practice file for these tasks is located in the MOSWordExpert2013\Objective2 practice file folder. Save the results of the tasks in the same folder.

- Open the *WordExpert_2-1* document, and do the following:
  - ○ Insert a continuous section break before the heading for section 1 and another before the heading for section 2.
  - ○ Define custom margins for the new section, specifying 1.5 inches for the top and bottom margins.
  - ○ Select the second and third paragraphs in section 1 and arrange the text in three columns. Adjust the spacing between columns 1 and 2 to 0.75 inches.
  - ○ Select the text in the columns, and then set the line spacing to exactly 10 points.
  - ○ In section 2, insert a picture from your computer or from an online source. Resize the picture, position it in the upper-right corner of the page, and then select the Tight text wrapping option.
  - ○ In section 3, link the text boxes. Delete or insert text in the first text box to observe how the text reflows.
  - ○ Select the title (*Layout practice*). Open the Font dialog box, and change the settings so that the title's character spacing is expanded by 1 point. Change the font to Gabriola, and apply one or more of the stylistic sets.
  - ○ Use the Find And Replace dialog box to locate words that end with the characters *lis*.
  - ○ Use the \n wildcard character to invert the phrase *Lorem ipsum*.
  - ○ At the top of the document, insert the Comments field from the Field dialog box and format the field so that the comment appears all uppercase.

2.2 Apply advanced styles

Every paragraph in a Word document is assigned a particular style. You can create an entire document that uses only the default Normal style and then format the text and other elements by adding bold or italic, increasing or decreasing font size, applying different fonts, and adding text effects. But even in a document that contains only one or two levels of headings and regular paragraphs of text, you need to do a lot of work to make elements of the same type consistent. Styles provide much more control and consistency in how the elements of a document appear, and after you apply styles to your document, you can change style properties once and Word updates the styles throughout the document.

> **Tip** To easily check which style is applied to each paragraph in a document, switch to Draft or Outline view. (You might need to increase the width of the style area pane, which you can do in the Word Options dialog box, in the Display section of the Advanced page.) Word also highlights the style applied to the selected paragraph in the Styles gallery.

This section describes how to create and modify styles, including character-specific styles you use to format particular words or single characters within a paragraph. This section also explains how to define shortcuts for applying styles from the keyboard.

Customizing settings for existing styles

The basic settings that define a style include font properties (font, size, and color), formatting such as bold or italic, text alignment (centered, flush left, flush right, or justified), line spacing, spacing between paragraphs, and indentation. Style definitions can also include settings for character spacing, borders, and text effects such as shadows, text outlines, and fills.

By changing these settings, you can modify a built-in style or a style that's defined in the template a document is based on. The Modify Style dialog box lists a style's properties in the preview box.

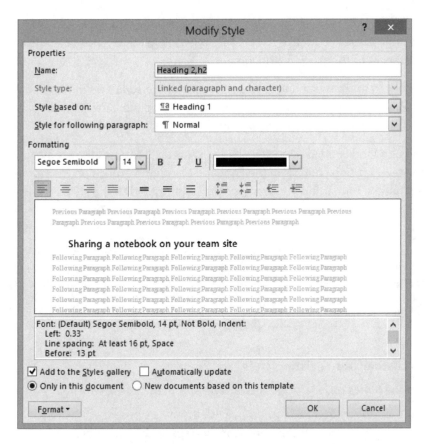

Many of a style's basic settings can be customized by using the controls in the Formatting area of the Modify Style dialog box. (These settings are roughly the same as the settings in the Font and Paragraph groups on the Home tab.) The Format button at the bottom of the dialog box opens a menu with commands that lead to dialog boxes you can use to refine settings for basic elements, including font and paragraph settings, and also to define or update settings for borders, frames, list formats, and special text effects.

When you modify a style, be sure to review the check boxes and option buttons at the bottom of the Modify Style dialog box. Keep Add To Styles Gallery selected if you have renamed a style and want to add it to the Styles gallery on the Home tab. Select

Automatically Update only if you want to automatically update a style's definition with formatting changes you make to text the style is applied to. Those changes are reflected in all instances of the style in a document.

If you want to make the changes to a style part of the style's definition in the associated template, select New Documents Based On This Template. Keep Only In This Document selected if that's the scope you're working with.

You can also modify an existing style by selecting text that uses the style and then formatting the text by using controls in the Font and Paragraph groups on the Home tab. When the text has the formatting you want for the style, right-click the style's name in the Styles gallery (or the Styles pane), and then click Update *Style Name* To Match Selection.

> **Tip** In the Word Options dialog box, in the Editing section on the Advanced page, select Prompt To Update Style to have Word display a dialog box when you apply a style from the Styles gallery that includes updated formatting. In the dialog box, Word prompts you to update the style to include the recent changes or to reapply the formatting defined in the style.

➤ **To customize an existing style**

1. In the **Styles** gallery, right-click a style and then choose **Modify**.

2. In the **Modify Style** dialog box, revise the style's properties by changing the font, specific font attributes, indentation, line space, and other settings.

3. For more detailed settings, click **Format**, and then choose the command for the element you want to format—**Paragraph**, **Font**, **Border**, or other elements.

4. To save the changes to this style to the current template, select **New documents based on this template**.

5. Click **OK**.

Creating custom styles

When you create a style, you work in the Create New Style From Formatting dialog box, which provides the same group of settings as the Modify Style dialog box. If you select and format existing text to include the style settings you want, the Create New Style From Formatting dialog box displays those settings when you open it. Use the controls in the Formatting area and the options on the Format menu to further define the style's attributes.

In the Properties area of the Create New Style From Formatting dialog box, you define the new style's name, the style type, which style the new style is based on, and the style Word applies automatically to a paragraph that follows the paragraph the new style is applied to.

- **Style type** The types of styles are paragraph, character, linked, table, and list. A linked style is a special case. When you select a linked style, Word applies the character formatting defined in a style (font color, for example, but not line spacing) or the style's full definition depending on what is selected in the document. When one or more words are selected, selecting a linked style applies the style's character formatting. Text that isn't selected is not changed and keeps the current paragraph formatting. If you select the paragraph or place the insertion point within the paragraph, a linked style applies both the character and paragraph settings defined in the style.

> **See Also** For details about character styles, see the "Creating character-specific styles" topic later in this section.

- **Style based on** Select a style whose properties you want to use as the basis for the new style. If you base a style on the built-in Normal style, for example, and then change the font for the Normal style from Calibri to Garamond, Word also changes the font for styles based on Normal to Garamond.

- **Style for following paragraph** Select the style for paragraphs that follow paragraphs that use this style. Word assigns that style when you insert a paragraph break by pressing Enter. For example, for a heading style, specify Normal or another body text style in this list.

➤ **To create a custom style**

1. Click the **Styles** dialog box launcher in the lower-right corner of the **Styles** group.

2. At the bottom of the **Styles** pane, click **New Style**.

3. In the **Create New Style from Formatting** dialog box, define the style's properties (name, type, and others), and then specify the font, font attributes, indentation, line space, and other settings that the style will apply.

4. For more detailed settings, click **Format**, and then choose the command for the element you want to format—**Paragraph**, **Font**, **Border**, and other elements.

5. To save the changes to this style to the current template, select **New documents based on this template**.

6. Click **OK**.

Creating character-specific styles

In many cases, you can capture all the formatting details you need in a paragraph style—indentation, font size, line spacing, and other such details. Within a paragraph, you can format characters by using the controls in the Font group on the Home tab or by choosing options in the Font dialog box. For more control over character formatting, you can also create styles specifically for groups of characters and then apply those styles as you format the document.

When you select Character in the Style Type list in the Create New Style From Formatting dialog box, the options in the dialog box change so that they apply only to character styles.

Character styles use only
font properties in their definitions

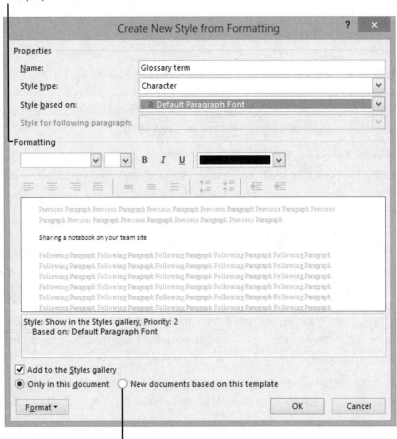

Select this option to add the style
to the current template

In the Style Based On list, Word displays Default Paragraph Font. Open the Style Based On list, and then choose from among the built-in character styles if you want to use one of them as a starting point. In the Formatting area of the dialog box, only controls related to character formatting are available to define the style.

➤ **To define a character style**

1. On the **Home** tab, click the dialog box launcher in the **Styles** group.
2. At the bottom of the **Styles** pane, click **New Style**.
3. In the **Create New Style from Formatting** dialog box, select **Character** in the **Style type** list.
4. Use the controls in the **Formatting** area to define the attributes for the style.

Assigning keyboard shortcuts to styles

Applying styles by using keyboard shortcuts helps you format a document as you enter the document's text and other content. Word provides the keyboard shortcuts for several of its built-in styles.

Style	Shortcut
Normal	Ctrl+Shift+N
Heading 1	Alt+Ctrl+1
Heading 2	Alt+Ctrl+2
Heading 3	Alt+Ctrl+3

You can assign your own keyboard shortcut to a style when you create it or when you modify the style's properties. In the Create New Style From Formatting or Modify Style dialog box, you can open the Customize Keyboard dialog box from the Format menu.

> **Tip** You can also open the Customize Keyboard dialog box from the Customize Ribbon page of the Word Options dialog box. In the Customize Keyboard dialog box, select Styles in the Categories list and then select the style you want to work with.

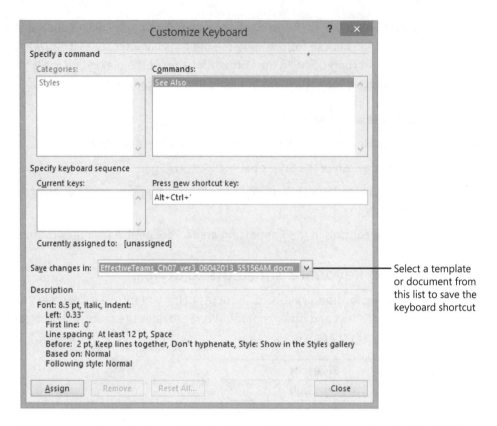

Select a template or document from this list to save the keyboard shortcut

When you assign a keyboard shortcut to a style, you can save the shortcut in the current template (including Normal.dotm, which makes the shortcut available to any document) or only in the document you are working in. The shortcut sequence must include Ctrl or Alt as the first key (you can include both keys) and at least one other of the character keys (A–Z, 1–9, and punctuation and special characters). You can include Shift in the sequence to extend the range of combinations. You can also include function keys (F1–F12), although these keys are usually already assigned to other operations. Word indicates whether a specific combination is already defined and what style or other operation it is assigned to when you enter a key combination.

➤ **To assign a keyboard shortcut to a style**

1. In the **Modify Style** dialog box, click **Format**, and then click **Shortcut Key**.

2. In the **Customize Keyboard** dialog box, click in the **Press new shortcut key** box.

3. On the keyboard, press the shortcut key sequence.

4. Click **Assign**, and then click **Close**.

Practice tasks

The practice file for these tasks is located in the MOSWordExpert2013\Objective2 practice file folder. Save the results of the tasks in the same folder.

- Open the *WordExpert_2-2* document, and do the following:
  - ○ Modify the Book Extract style to remove the hanging first line and the font color.
  - ○ Create a style named *Author Bio* and a style named *Back Matter Title*. Use formatting of your own choosing. Scroll to the end of the document and apply these styles to the About the Author section.
  - ○ Create a character-specific style named *Glossary Term*. Use bold and a dark blue font color as the style's main attributes. Apply the style to the document where the Emphasis style is currently applied.
  - ○ Assign a keyboard shortcut to the Back Matter Title style you created earlier in this set of tasks.

2.3 Apply advanced ordering and grouping

This section describes two approaches for organizing and managing longer documents: outlines and master documents. This section also describes how to link elements of a document for ease of navigation.

Creating and managing outlines

An outline is a hierarchical structure that you can use to organize long documents, reports, and presentations. In Word, you can use the built-in heading styles (Heading 1 through Heading 9) to organize an outline. (An outline does not need to include levels for each heading style.) Headings are assigned a level that reflects their position in the hierarchy—main headings, subheadings, and sub-subheadings.

In Outline view, Word provides tools for creating, displaying, and organizing an outline. Outline view also shows the outline's hierarchy by slightly indenting each level of heading. You can also create an outline in Print Layout view, Draft view, or Web Layout view. The Multilevel List command in the Paragraph group on the Home tab provides built-in options for outline styles and an option you can use to define a custom multilevel-list style.

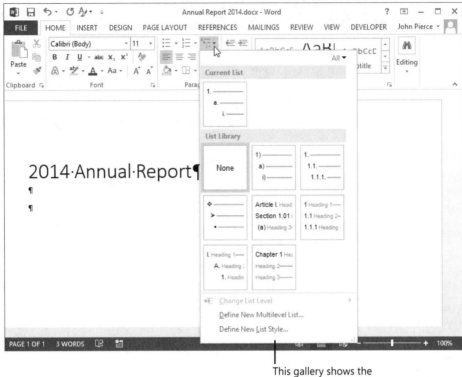

This gallery shows the
built-in styles for outlines

Tip If you create a single-level numbered list by using the automatic numbered list feature, you can convert the list to an outline. Select an item in the list, click the arrow next to Numbering in the Paragraph group on the Home tab, click Change List Level, and then click the outline level for that item.

In Page Layout, Web Layout, or Draft view, open the Navigation pane to display the headings in a document in outline form. Right-click a heading to adjust a heading's level, add headings and subheadings to the document, delete a heading, and adjust the view of the outline so that you display the headings only to a specific level.

When you create an outline in Outline view, the first line you enter is styled as Heading 1 and is assigned to Level 1 in the outline's hierarchy. As you continue entering headings and content, you work with options on the Outline Tools group to promote and demote sections in the outline, refine the outline's order by moving sections up or down, and expand or collapse the view of the outline to display only headings, or headings and the content in each section. You can also view only specific levels in the outline.

Use these controls to promote and demote headings
Use these controls to move sections of an outline
and to expand or collapse selected sections

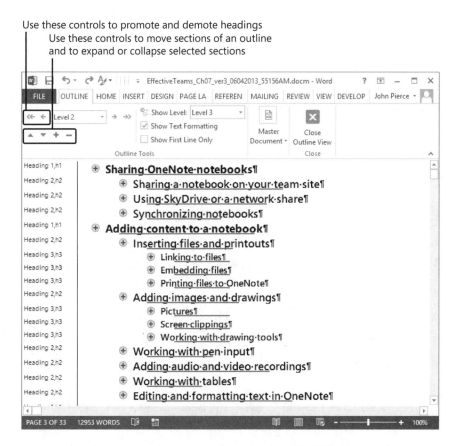

To manage the view and organization of an outline, Word provides a set of keyboard shortcuts.

Action	Keyboard shortcut
Switch to Outline view	Ctrl+Alt+O
Show Level 1 headings only	Alt+Shift+1
Show headings to Level 2	Alt+Shift+2
Show headings to Level 3	Alt+Shift+3
Show headings to Level 4	Alt+Shift+4
Show headings to Level 5	Alt+Shift+5
Show headings to Level 6	Alt+Shift+6
Show headings to Level 7	Alt+Shift+7
Show headings to Level 8	Alt+Shift+8
Show headings to Level 9	Alt+Shift+9

Action	Keyboard shortcut
Promote by one level	Shift+Tab or Alt+Shift+Left Arrow
Demote by one level	Tab or Alt+Shift+Right Arrow
Expand a collapsed outline	Alt+Shift+Plus Sign
Collapse an expanded outline	Alt+Shift+Minus Sign
Move up	Alt+Shift+Up Arrow
Move down	Alt+Shift+Down Arrow

> **To create an outline in Outline view**

1. Create a blank document or a document based on a template.

2. On the **View** tab, in the **Views** group, click **Outline**.

3. Enter the headings in the document, and use the **Outline Level** list to assign an outline level to each entry.

> **To manage an outline in Outline view**

→ Switch to **Outline** view, and then do any of the following:

   ○ To promote a heading in the outline (making a subheading a main heading), select the heading, and then click **Promote** in the **Outline Tools** group.

   ○ To demote a heading, select the heading, and then click **Demote** in the **Outline Tools** group.

   ○ To move a section within the outline, select the section heading, and then click **Move Up** or **Move Down** in the **Outline Tools** group.

   ○ To change the view of an outline, click **Expand** or **Collapse** in the **Outline Tools** group.

   ○ To view headings at a specific level and above, in the **Show Level** list, select the level you want to view.

> **To create an outline by using a built-in multilevel list style**

1. On the **Home** tab, click **Multilevel List**, and then click the style you want to use.

2. Enter a top-level heading, and then press **Enter**.

3. Press **Tab** to enter a heading at level 2.

4. Continuing entering the outline headings. Press **Tab** to add a heading at a subordinate level, or press **Shift+Tab** to move up a level in the outline hierarchy.

Creating master documents

A master document is a container for other documents, called *subdocuments*. You can set up a master document to help manage a set of related documents that have a common table of contents, a sequence of figures or tables, a set of cross-references, footnotes or endnotes, or an index. Creating a master document and subdocuments can also be used when a group of people are working together on a multipart document. Members of the group can work independently on separate subdocuments. In addition, by using a master document, you can search for and replace text within the master document instead of performing this operation in each of the subdocuments.

The Master Document group on the ribbon appears on the Outlining tab that Word displays in Outline view. Click Show Document in the Master Document group to display the commands you use to build a master document and manage the subdocuments it contains.

The Master Document commands on the ribbon are:

- **Show Document** Shows or hides master document commands (except for Collapse Subdocuments).

- **Collapse Subdocuments** Controls the display of subdocuments, showing only the name and path of subdocuments or showing the full subdocuments (text, images, and other content).

- **Create** Creates subdocuments from selected headings in an outline. Using the top-level headings in the selected sections, Word creates separate files to serve as the subdocuments.

- **Insert** Inserts a file into the master document as a subdocument.

- **Unlink** Deletes the link between the subdocument and the master document and copies the contents of the subdocument to the master document.

- **Merge** Combines selected subdocuments into a single subdocument. The new subdocument uses the name of the first subdocument in the selection.

- **Split** Splits a subdocument into additional subdocuments at the next lower heading level.

- **Lock Document** Determines whether a subdocument can be modified or is read-only.

You can create a master document by inserting existing documents as the subdocuments or by converting a document with an outline structure into a master document and subdocuments. When you insert existing files into a master document, if the document you are inserting uses a different template from the master document, Word informs you that the master document's template will be used. Word also prompts you to rename each style that exists in both documents. You aren't required to rename any of the subdocument's styles. Click No if you want to preserve the style's name. If you choose to have Word rename the style, Word adds 1 to the style's name.

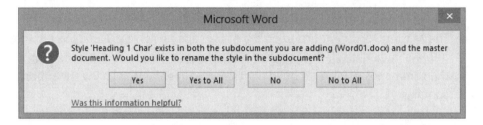

Converting a document entails using Outline view and selecting which sections of a document you want Word to convert to subdocuments. Word creates the new subdocuments when you save the master document.

➤ **To create a master document from an existing document**

1. Create a blank document.

2. On the **View** tab, click **Outline**.

3. On the **Outlining** tab, click **Show Document**.

4. In the **Master Document** group, click **Insert.**

5. In the **Insert Subdocument** dialog box, select the file you want to insert, and then click **Open**.

6. If prompted, click **OK** in the dialog box informing you that Word will use the master document's template.

7. In the dialog box Word displays, click **Yes** (or **Yes to All**) or **No** (or **No to All**) to specify whether Word should rename styles.

8. Repeat steps 4 through 7 to insert additional files as subdocuments.

➤ **To convert a document to a master document and subdocuments**

1. Open the document, and then, on the **View** tab, click **Outline**.

2. On the **Outlining** tab, click **Show Document**.

3. In the outline, select the section or sections you want to convert to subdocuments.

4. In the **Master Document** group, click **Create**.

5. Save the master document.

Linking document elements

Moving from section to section in a long document can require lots of scrolling, and as you scroll you need to browse the document to find the text or section you are looking for.

You can take a couple of approaches to making navigation easier. One is to open the Navigation pane to display a document's headings. Click a heading in the Navigation pane to jump to that heading in a document.

> **Note** The Navigation pane also provides a search box that you can use to quickly search for a word or phrase in your document.

Another way to link sections in a document is to use bookmarks and hyperlinks. To set up these links, you use commands in the Links group on the Insert tab. You can define a bookmark for section headings, subheadings, or other document elements. Keep in mind that names for the bookmark cannot include any spaces.

If you want to go one step further, you can create a hyperlink to a bookmark, possibly from a document's table of contents. In the Insert Hyperlink dialog box, use the Place In This Document option to specify the bookmark or heading you want to link to.

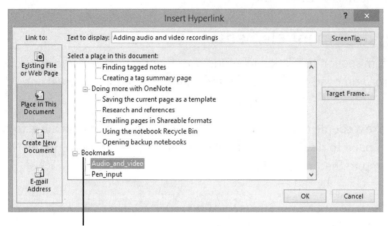

Select a bookmark here to create
a link to that place in the document

> **To link document sections**

1. Select the text you want to link to, and then click **Bookmark** on the **Insert** tab.

2. In the **Bookmark** dialog box, name the bookmark, and then click **Add**.

3. Select the place in the document where you want to insert a hyperlink to the bookmark.

4. On the **Insert** tab, click **Hyperlink**.

5. In the **Insert Hyperlink** dialog box, select **Place in this Document**.

6. Select the bookmark to link to, and then click **OK**.

> **To move to a bookmark**

1. On the **Home** tab, click the **Find** arrow, and then click **Go To**.

2. In the **Find and Replace** dialog box, in the **Go to what** list, select **Bookmark**.

3. Select the bookmark, and then click **Go To**.

Practice tasks

The practice files for these tasks are located in the MOSWordExpert2013\
Objective2 practice file folder. Save the results of the tasks in the same folder.

- Open the *WordExpert_2-3a* document, and do the following:

  - Switch to Outline view, and the use the headings in the file—which are based on topics in this chapter—to create an outline that matches the organization and order of this chapter.

- Open the *WordExpert_2-3b* document, and do the following:

  - Create a master document by creating subdocuments based on sections 2.1, 2.2, and 2.3.

- Create a blank document, switch to Outline view, display the master document tools, and then do the following:

  - Create a master document by inserting the *WordExpert_2-3c*, *WordExpert_2-3d*, and *WordExpert_2-3e* documents. (You can also use files of your own.)

Objective review

Before finishing this chapter, ensure that you have mastered the following skills:

2.1   Apply advanced formatting

2.2   Apply advanced styles

2.3   Apply advanced ordering and grouping

3 Create advanced references

The skills tested in this section of the Microsoft Office Specialist Expert exams for Microsoft Word 2013 relate to creating advanced references, including indexes and tables of contents. Specifically, the following objectives are associated with this set of skills:

3.1 Create and manage indexes

3.2 Create and manage reference tables

3.3 Manage forms, fields, and mail merge operations

This chapter guides you in studying the mechanics of creating and managing different types of reference material you can include in a document, including indexes, tables of contents, and tables of authorities. Most of the tools you use for these tasks appear on the References tab. This chapter also explains how to design forms by using content controls such as text boxes and list boxes, how to use fields to display and manage information, and how to set up and run a mail merge operation.

> **Practice Files** To complete the practice tasks in this chapter, you need the practice files contained in the MOSWordExpert2013\Objective3 practice file folder. For more information, see "Download the practice files" in this book's Introduction.

3.1 Create and manage indexes

To create an index in a document, you need to complete two general steps: mark index entries (by inserting a type of field) in the document and set options for how Word generates the index. Word uses the entries and the options you specify to create the index, assigning page numbers to entries on the basis of their location throughout the document.

You can follow any of several approaches for marking index entries. You can select text in a document to use as an entry, insert an entry of your own where you want the index marker to appear, or insert index markers by using a list of terms set up in a separate file, which Word uses to scan the document you are indexing and insert index markers automatically.

An index entry must have at least one level, the *main entry*. Index entries can also include *subentries* and *cross-references* to other entries in the index. Entries can refer to a specific page or to a range of pages.

An example of a main entry is *styles*, which might include subentries such as *applying*, *creating*, and *updating in template*. The page reference for the main entry might span several pages in this example, with subentries covered on a single page or a span of fewer pages.

Marking index entries

When you insert entries manually, you work in the Mark Index Entry dialog box. If text is selected when you open the Mark Index Entry dialog box, that text appears in the Main Entry box. You can keep the Mark Index Entry dialog box open as you work on a document. Text that is selected when you click the dialog box to make it active replaces any text currently contained in the Main Entry box. You don't need to select text to create a main entry, however. You can define a main entry yourself by placing the cursor where you want an index reference in the document and then entering the text in the Main Entry box.

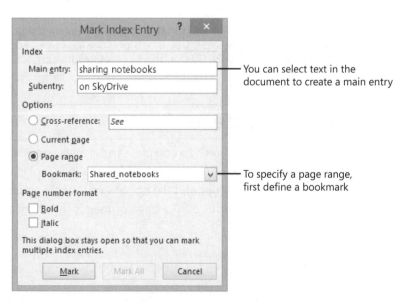

You can select text in the document to create a main entry

To specify a page range, first define a bookmark

> **Tip** You can apply formatting such as bold or italic to the text in the Main Entry, Subentry, and Cross-Reference boxes.

Subentries for a main entry must be entered manually. You can create a third-level entry by entering a colon (:) after the subentry and then the text of the third-level entry. In the Options area, you can create a cross-reference (a *See* reference) to other index entries as applicable.

Word uses a field to define index entries. An index field is identified by the characters *XE* and encloses all the information for an entry in curly braces. Index fields are displayed in hidden text. If the index fields are not displayed in your document, click Show/Hide ¶ (the paragraph icon) in the Paragraph group on the Home tab, or press Ctrl+Shift+8.

Here is an example of the information that an index field might contain:

{ XE "formatting:characters: font" \t See also styles" }

Entries that span a range of pages refer to bookmarks defined in the document. Select the paragraphs in the range you want to use, and then use the Bookmark dialog box to define the bookmark. In the Mark Index Entry dialog box, choose Page Range and then select the bookmark you defined for that range. Use the options provided for formatting the page number in bold or italic.

The Mark All button in the Mark Index Entry dialog box inserts an index field for each occurrence of the main entry in the document. For example, if the main entry is *styles*, clicking Mark All inserts an index field for each occurrence of the word *styles* in the document.

Building indexes from automark files

Another method for building the list of entries for an index is to list main entries in a separate document (also referred to as an *automark file* or a *concordance file*) that Word uses to mark your document. The automark file can be saved as a Word document or in other formats, such as a text (.txt) file.

You can set up the entries in a single-level list, in which case Word searches for each term or phrase in the list and inserts a corresponding index field for each instance of the term or phrase it finds. For more flexibility, you can set up the list in a two-column table, with the terms you want to search for in the left column and the corresponding index entries in the right column. By using two columns, you can collect terms such as *format, formatting,* and *formatted* under the same main entry—list the terms separately in the left column and associate them with the same main entry in the table's right column. The entries in an automark file are case-sensitive. For example, if the auto-mark file includes the term *text effects*, Word won't insert an index field for an instance of *Text effects* when it indexes the document.

Inserting indexes

After you mark index entries, you use the Index dialog box to set up the index's design and specify other options.

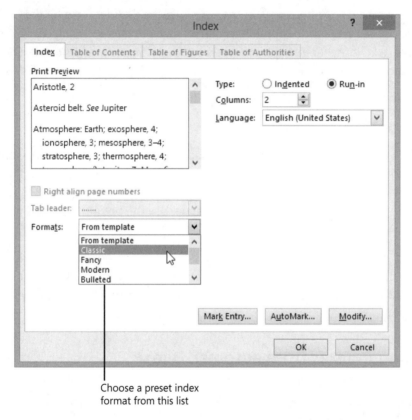

Choose a preset index
format from this list

Word supports two index formats: indented and run-in. In a run-in index, main entries and subentries are formatted as follows:

Styles: applying, 211; creating, 209; updating
  in template, 212

In an indented index, the entries are listed in this format:

Styles
  applying, 211
  creating, 209
  updating in template, 212

When the length of an index is a factor, you can use a run-in index to save space. When you select an option for the type of index, Word displays an example in the Print Preview area of the Index dialog box.

By default, Word creates a two-column index. You can choose the Auto setting or specify from one to four columns. If you are setting up an indented index, you can change the alignment of page numbers. Word previews this format when you select the option, and you can then select the type of tab leader you want to include (or select None from this list). The Formats list provides several options for styling the fonts, line spacing, and other formats Word applies to the index entries when you generate the index.

> **Tip** If From Template is selected in the Formats list, you can modify the styles for index levels. Click Modify in the Index dialog box. In the Styles dialog box, select an index level, and then click Modify to open the Modify Style dialog box and make changes to the formatting attributes for that index level. For more information about modifying styles, see section 2.2, "Apply advanced styles."

Editing and updating indexes

If you need to edit an index entry, you should edit the specific index field and not the index that Word generates. Locate the field in the document, and then edit and format the text enclosed in quotation marks within the curly braces that define the field. To delete an index marker, select the field (including the braces) and press the Delete key.

After you make changes to index markers, use the Update Index command on the References tab to generate the index again.

> **Tip** When you need to edit an index, use the Find And Replace dialog box to move from field to field. In the dialog box, click Special (click More if the Special button isn't displayed), and then select Field. Click Find Next to move to the first field. To continue from field to field, click Find Next again, or close the dialog box and press Shift+F4.

➤ **To mark index entries**

1. On the **References** tab, in the **Index** group, click **Mark Entry**.

2. In the document, select the text for a main entry, and then click the **Mark Index Entry** dialog box to make it active.

Or

Position the cursor where you want a reference to appear in the document, and then enter the entry in the **Main Entry** box.

3. In the **Subentry** box, enter a subentry. To define a third-level entry, add a colon to the end of the subentry, and then enter the third-level entry.

4. In the **Options** area, do one of the following:

   ○ Click **Cross-reference**, and then enter the text for the reference.

   ○ Click **Current page**.

   ○ Click **Page range**, and then select the bookmark for the range of pages the entry is related to. (See the next procedure for the steps you follow to create a bookmark.)

5. In the **Page number format** area, select bold and italic formatting as required.

6. Click **Mark**, or click **Mark All** to mark all instances of this entry in the document.

➤ **To define a bookmark for a page range**

1. Select the paragraphs you want to include in the page range.

2. On the **Insert** tab, in the **Links** group, click **Bookmark**.

3. In the **Bookmark** dialog box, enter a name for the bookmark, and then click **Add**.

➤ **To mark index entries by using an automark file**

1. Create the automark file by using a list or a two-column table.

2. On the **References** tab, in the **Index** group, click **Insert Index**.

3. In the **Index** dialog box, click **AutoMark**.

4. In the **Open Index AutoMark File** dialog box, select the file, and then click **Open**.

➤ **To specify index formatting options and generate the index**

1. In the document, place your cursor where you want the index to appear.

2. On the **References** tab, in the **Index** group, click **Insert Index**.

3. In the **Index** dialog box, set any of the following options:

   ○ Select a type of index: indented or run-in.

   ○ Specify the number of columns.

   ○ Choose a language if you are using a language other than the default language on your system.

○ If you are using an indented index, click **Right align page numbers**, and then select the style of tab leader you want to use.

○ Select a format for the index, or keep **From template** selected.

4. Click **OK**.

➤ **To edit and update an index**

1. In the document, click **Show/Hide ¶** if the index fields are not displayed.

2. Select the text in the field for the entry you want to edit, and then revise and format the entry.

3. Place the cursor in the index, and then, on the **References** tab, click **Update Index**.

Practice tasks

The practice files for these tasks are located in the MOSWordExpert2013\
Objective3 practice file folder. Save the results of the tasks in the same folder.

- Open the *WordExpert_3-1a* document. Work through the file, adding index entries for terms such as *formatting, styles, templates,* and others. Add sub-entries for several main entries (such as *styles, modifying*), and define a page range by using a bookmark. Generate the index, and then edit a handful of entries by using the field tags. Update the index to reflect your changes.

- Create an automark file by using the terms from the previous practice task. Use the file to insert an index in the *WordExpert_3-1b* document.

3.2 Create and manage reference tables

Research and scholarly documents, and also many types of legal and business documents, include citations to sources that the authors of the documents referred to. The References tab provides tools that you can use to build a list of sources by using the information required by conventional authorities such as the Modern Language Association or the *Chicago Manual of Style*. You can manage these sources, insert the citations where you need them in a document, and when the citations are in place, create a bibliography or a list of works cited.

Word also provides mechanisms for creating and managing other types of references, including tables of contents, tables of figures, and footnotes and endnotes. This section describes how you create and update reference tables, citations, and notes.

Creating and formatting tables of contents

Word can use its built-in heading styles and other styles you specify to create a table of contents. With these styles in place in a document, you can use the Table Of Contents gallery on the References tab to insert a table of contents. The gallery provides two built-in formats: one uses the title *Contents*, and the second the more formal *Table of Contents*. The second option also inserts a page break.

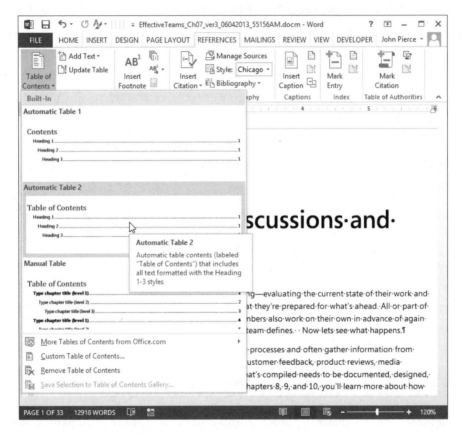

The Manual Table option in the gallery inserts placeholders for a table of contents with three levels. Use this option if you want to build a table of contents from scratch.

A built-in table of contents that is tied to styles can easily be updated. You can edit the headings in the body of the document and then regenerate the table of contents. You don't need to edit the headings in both locations.

The Table Of Contents dialog box (which Word displays if you click Custom Table Of Contents at the bottom of the gallery) provides a set of options for which levels of headings Word includes in the table of contents, and also formatting options.

Clear this check box if you don't
need hyperlinks in the document

Click Modify to change the style
for entries in a table of contents

By default, Word includes three levels of headings in a table of contents. You can display as few as one and as many as nine of the built-in heading styles. In the Formats list, you can select a built-in format or keep the default setting From Template. As in the Index dialog box, when From Template is selected, you can click the Modify button to open the Styles dialog box, where you can select one of the built-in table of contents (TOC) styles for modification.

The Options button in the Table Of Contents dialog box opens a dialog box in which you can designate other styles and specify additional options for elements that Word includes in the table of contents. The styles listed in the dialog box depend on the template applied to the document.

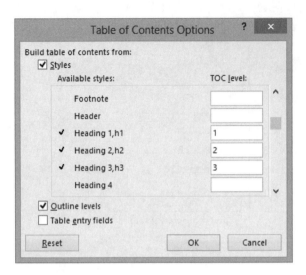

In the Table Of Contents Options dialog box, check marks indicate styles Word uses to create the table of contents and the level each style is associated with. You can include other styles in the table of contents by specifying a level in the TOC Level list. For example, to include sidebar headings as a fourth-level entry in a table of contents, enter 4 in the TOC Level list for the style Sidebar Heading.

By default, Word also uses outline levels to create a table of contents. You can assign an outline level to a style when you create or modify the style. For example, you might assign an outline level to a style you create for sidebar headings or captions so that you can view the content associated with these styles when you display a document in Outline view. When you insert a table of contents, however, you probably won't want Word to include these styles. Clear the Outline Levels check box when that's the case.

> **See Also** For details about working with outlines, see section 2.3, "Apply advanced ordering and grouping."

The Table Entry Fields check box in the Table Of Contents Options dialog box refers to headings or other elements of a document that have been manually marked to be included in the table of contents. You can create an entry by selecting the text, pressing Alt+Shift+O to open the Mark Table Of Contents Entry dialog box, setting the level, and then clicking Mark. To include the manual entries in the table of contents, you need to select this check box before you generate the table.

> **Tip** You can use the Add Text tool in the Table Of Contents group on the References tab to change the style applied to headings in a document. The Add Text tool displays the command Do Not Show In Table Of Contents and a list of numbers that match the settings in the TOC Level list in the Table Of Contents dialog box (1, 2, and 3, by default). You can, for example, apply the Heading 1 style to a paragraph formatted as Heading 2 by selecting the paragraph and then clicking 1 on the Add Text menu. If you select Do Not Show In Table Of Contents, Word applies the Normal style to the heading.

➤ **To insert a built-in table of contents**

1. In the document, apply the built-in heading styles (Heading 1 through Heading 3) to the elements you want to include in the table of contents.

2. Place the cursor where you want the table of contents to appear.

3. On the **References** tab, click **Table of Contents**.

4. In the **Table of Contents** gallery, click **Automatic Table 1** or **Automatic Table 2**.

➤ **To build a table of contents from scratch**

1. Place the cursor where you want the table of contents to appear.

2. On the **References** tab, click **Table of Contents**.

3. In the **Table of Contents** gallery, click **Manual Table**.

4. In the placeholders Word inserts, enter the headings for levels you want to include. To insert additional placeholders, copy and paste a blank placeholder.

➤ **To create a custom table of contents**

1. Place the cursor where you want the table of contents to appear.

2. On the **References** tab, click **Table of Contents**.

3. In the **Table of Contents** gallery, click **Custom Table of Contents**.

4. In the **Table of Contents** dialog box, set options for showing and aligning page numbers, and choose the tab leader character and a table of contents format.

5. To change which heading levels appear in the table of contents, specify the number in the **Show Levels** list.

6. To remove hyperlinks from the table of contents headings, clear the **Use hyperlinks instead of page numbers** check box.

7. Click **OK** to insert the table of contents.

➤ **To set options for a table of contents**

1. Place the cursor where you want the table of contents to appear.

2. On the **References** tab, click **Table of Contents**, and then click **Custom Table of Contents**.

3. In the **Table of Contents** dialog box, click **Options**.

4. In the **Table of Contents Options** dialog box, do any of the following:

   ○ To include other styles in the table of contents, specify the level in the **TOC Level** box to the right of the style's name.

   ○ To exclude outline levels from the table of contents, clear the **Outline levels** check box.

   ○ To exclude styled elements from the table of contents, clear the **Styles** check box, and then use outline levels or table entry fields.

   ○ To include manually marked table entries, select the **Table entry fields** check box.

5. Click **OK** in the **Table of Contents Options** dialog box, and then click **OK** in the **Table of Contents** dialog box.

➤ **To update a table of contents**

1. Place the cursor in the table of contents.

2. On the **References** tab, in the **Table of Contents** group, click **Update Table**.

➤ **To remove a table of contents**

1. Place the cursor in the table of contents.

2. On the **References** tab, click **Table of Contents**, and then click **Remove Table of Contents**.

Creating tables of figures

Another type of reference table is a table of figures. Word generates a table of figures from captions you associate with illustrations and other types of objects, such as tables, charts, or diagrams. You can add captions to a variety of elements in a document.

Inserting captions

The first step in creating a table of figures is to insert captions. The Insert Caption command in the Captions group opens a dialog box in which you enter a caption and define settings for how Word displays it.

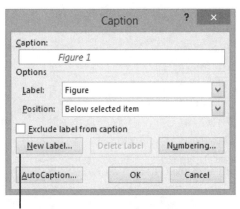

Click New Label to create additional
labels for items for which you want a caption

In the Caption dialog box, use the Label list to select the type of object you are adding a
caption to (a figure, in this example). The default choices are equation, figure, and table.
You can define captions for other types of objects (charts, for example) by clicking New
Label. (You can delete custom labels when you no longer need them, but you cannot
delete the default labels.)

Click the Numbering button to display the Caption Numbering dialog box, and then use
this dialog box to switch to a different numbering format or to include a chapter number
with a caption's label. Chapter headings must be defined by using one of Word's built-in
heading styles.

> **Tip** If you insert a particular type of object repeatedly in a document and you want these
> objects to have a caption, click AutoCaption in the Caption dialog box. Select the type of
> object (Bitmap Image or Microsoft Excel Worksheet, for example) that you want Word
> to provide a caption for when you insert an object of this type. You can adjust the label
> that's used with a particular type of object, where Word positions the caption by default,
> and how the captions are numbered.

Inserting tables of figures

The steps and options for creating a table of figures are similar to those for a table of
contents. The Table Of Figures dialog box previews how Word will display the table in
a printed document and online. You can choose a built-in format or use the style defined in the current template. For the caption label, you can select None, Figure, Table,
Equation, or a custom label you define by using the Caption dialog box.

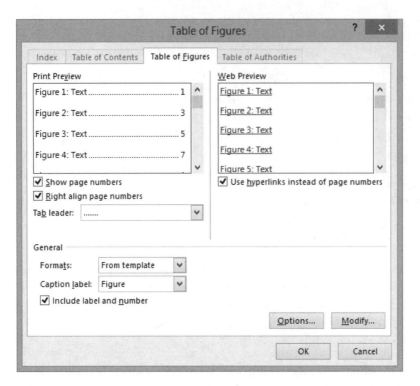

By default, Word uses its built-in Caption style and the associated label to build the table of figures. Any element to which that style is applied and that is labeled as a figure is included. In the Table Of Figures Options dialog box, you can select a different style or use table entries you define manually. As you can with table of content styles, you can modify the style Word uses to display the table of figures by selecting From Template in the Formats list, clicking Modify in the Table Of Figures dialog box, and then using the Styles dialog box and the Modify Style dialog box to update the style's attributes.

➤ **To create a caption for a document element**

1. Select the object you want to create a caption for.

2. On the **References** tab, in the **Captions** group, click **Insert Caption**.

3. In the **Caption** dialog box, in the **Label** list, select the type of object, and then enter the caption after the label in the **Caption** box.

4. In the **Position** list, select an option for where you want the caption to appear.

5. Click **Numbering** to open the **Caption Numbering** dialog box, and then adjust number formatting for the caption.

6. Click **OK** in the **Caption Numbering** dialog box, and then click **OK** in the **Caption** dialog box.

➤ **To create a custom label**

1. On the **References** tab, in the **Captions** group, click **Insert Captions**.

2. In the **Caption** dialog box, click **New Label**.

3. Enter a name for the label, and then click **OK**.

➤ **To insert a table of figures**

1. Place the cursor where you want the table of figures to appear.

2. On the **References** tab, click **Insert Table of Figures**.

3. In the **Table of Figures** dialog box, set options for showing and aligning page numbers and choose the tab leader character and a table of figures format.

4. In the **Caption label** list, select the label you want to include with the captions.

5. To remove hyperlinks from the table of figure entries, clear the **Use hyperlinks instead of page numbers** check box.

6. Click **OK** to insert the table of figures.

➤ **To set options for a table of figures**

1. In the **Table of Figures** dialog box, click **Options**.

2. In the **Table of Figures Options** dialog box, do any of the following:

   ○ To base the table on a different style, select **Style**, and then choose a style from the list.

   ○ To include manually marked table entries, select **Table entry fields**.

3. Click **OK** in the **Table of Figures Options** dialog box, and then click **OK** in the **Table of Figures** dialog box to insert the table.

Working with tables of authorities

A table of authorities is used in legal documents as a reference to the cases, statutes, rulings, regulations, and other citations included in a document. Word can generate a table of authorities on the basis of the citations you mark and define in a document. The table of authorities feature in Word provides several built-in categories that you use to classify citations, but you can modify this list or add categories of your own. Word also provides options for formatting a table of authorities and for how the table displays the citations.

Marking citations

To start building a table of authorities, you mark entries by using the Mark Citation dialog box. Any text that you select before you open the dialog box (by clicking Mark

Citation in the Table Of Authorities group on the References tab) appears in the Selected Text box and the Short Citation box. You can edit the citation's text in the Selected Text box or in the Short Citation box. To format the citation, right-click in the Selected Text box, and then choose Font.

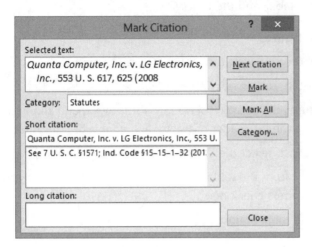

Word provides seven named categories by default (cases, statutes, other authorities, rules, treatises, regulations, and constitutional provisions), along with unspecified categories numbered 8 through 16. You can replace a named category or assign a name to a numbered category to modify what Word provides.

Select one of the numbered categories and assign a label to it

If you click Mark All in the Mark Citation dialog box, Word inserts a table of authorities field (identified by the characters *TA*) for each instance in the document that matches the text in the long and short forms you define. You can keep the Mark Citation dialog box open as you navigate through a document, to mark other citations. The Next Citation button moves to the next likely citation in the document—Word uses clues such as *v.* or dates in parentheses—for example, *(2001)*—to identify citations.

Formatting and inserting tables of authorities

When you're ready to build your table of authorities, you set options in the Table Of Authorities dialog box.

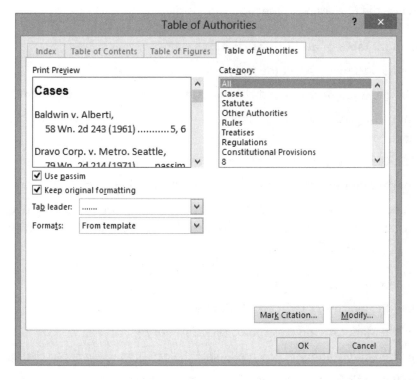

In the Table Of Authorities dialog box, you can set the following options:

- **Category** Select which category of authorities you want to include, or choose All. You cannot choose more than one option in this list.

- **Use passim** Keep this check box selected if you want to use the term *passim* to indicate that information the citation refers to is scattered throughout the source. Clear this check box to list specific pages for each citation.

- **Keep original formatting** Use this option to specify whether the citations listed in the table of authorities appear in the table as they are formatted in the document.

- **Tab leader** Choose the type of tab leader to use (which helps align page numbers), or choose None from this list.

- **Formats** Choose a style for the table of authorities, or use the styles and formatting that are defined in the current template.

To change formatting for the table of authorities entries and the table heading, use the From Template setting in the Formats list, and then click Modify to open the Styles dialog box. Select the element you want to change, click Modify in the Style dialog box, and then revise the formatting in the Modify Style dialog box.

➤ **To mark table of authorities citations**

1. In the document, select the text for a citation.
2. On the **References** tab, in the **Table of Authorities** group, click **Mark Citation**.
3. In the **Mark Citation** dialog box, edit the text for the citation in the **Selected text** box.
4. Edit the short form for the citation in the **Short citation** box.
5. In the **Category** list, select a category for the citation.
6. Click **Mark**, or click **Mark All**, to insert a table of authorities reference for each instance of this citation as you have defined it in the **Mark Citation** dialog box.
7. Click **Next Citation**, and repeat steps 3 through 6.

➤ **To define or replace a category for a table of authorities**

1. On the **References** tab, click **Mark Citation**.
2. In the **Mark Citation** dialog box, click **Category**.
3. In the **Edit Category** dialog box, select the category you want to change.
4. In the **Replace with** box, modify the category name.
5. Click **Replace**.
6. Make changes to other categories as necessary, and then click **OK**.

➤ **To format and generate a table of authorities**

1. Position the cursor where you want the table of authorities to appear in the document.

2. On the **References** tab, in the **Table of Authorities** group, click **Insert Table of Authorities**.

3. In the **Table of Authorities** dialog box, do any of the following:

   ○ Select the category of citation you want to create a table for, or select **All**.

   ○ Select the **Use Passim** check box to use the term *passim* for short-form references, or clear it to show specific page numbers referred to in the citation.

   ○ Select or clear the **Keep original formatting** check box to tell Word whether to maintain the formatting defined for the citation in the **Mark Citation** dialog box.

   ○ Select a tab leader to use to align page numbers.

   ○ Select a format for the table, or choose **From template**.

4. Click **OK**.

➤ **To update a table of authorities**

1. Place the cursor in the table.

2. On the **References** tab, in the **Table of Authorities** group, click **Update Table**.

Setting advanced reference options

This section describes additional aspects of working with references in a document. It covers cross-references, footnote and endnote options, and how to manage bibliographic references.

Using cross-references

Items that you label with a caption (figures, tables, and equations, for example)—as well as document elements such as numbered items, headings, bookmarks, and notes—can be cross-referenced in a document. Cross-references help you locate specific content and help keep the numbering of captioned objects up to date.

With the cursor positioned where you want to add a cross-reference, enter some text that introduces the object you are cross-referencing (for example, *For a summary of the amino acids analyzed, see*). In the Cross-Reference dialog box (which you open from the Captions group on the References tab), you then select the type of reference. For example, to reference a table, you select Table in the Reference Type list. Word then displays a list of tables labeled with a caption created in Word.

The Insert Reference To list provides options for how the reference appears—a page number, for example, or the text of a heading.

The selection in the Reference Type box determines what elements you can refer to here

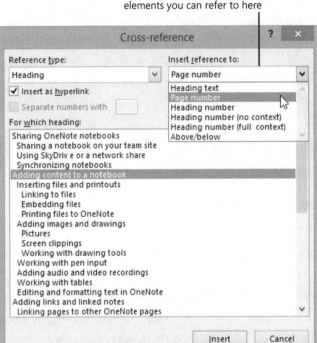

For some types of references (headings or bookmarks, for example), the Insert Reference To list includes two types of numbers: No Context and Full Context. These options are used with lists or outlines that use multiple levels. The Full Context option includes each element in a numbering scheme—for example, *4.1.1.a*. The No Context alternative refers only to the last of the levels used.

The Include Above/Below check box provides the option to insert a positional cross-reference that uses the word *above* or *below* depending on where the item you are referring to is located in relation to the reference.

Keep the Insert As Hyperlink check box selected if you want to create a hyperlink from the cross-reference to the reference's target. The hyperlinks you create in the Cross-Reference dialog box work in Word and in a browser, if you save a document as a webpage.

➤ **To insert a cross-reference**

1. Enter the text you want to use to introduce the item you are referencing.

2. On the **References** tab, in the **Captions** group, click **Cross-reference**.

3. In the **Cross-reference** dialog box, select the reference type.

4. In the **Insert reference to** list, select which option you want to use as the reference (page number, caption, or section heading, for example).

5. In the **For which** list, select the target for the cross-reference.

6. Click **Insert**.

Setting options for footnotes and endnotes

The use of notes (footnotes or endnotes) is required in many documents to provide attribution for sources of quotations, facts, and opinions. The References tab includes the Footnotes group. You use the Insert Footnote or Insert Endnote commands to add a note to your document. Footnotes appear at the bottom of a page, whereas endnotes appear at the end of a document or a section.

The settings for how footnotes and endnotes are displayed are controlled in the Footnote And Endnote dialog box, which Word displays when you click the dialog box launcher in the Footnotes group.

You can set options for where notes appear, for example, and the layout of footnotes (in columns or with the same layout as the current section). You can change the number format, specify a custom mark or symbol, specify the starting number, and designate whether numbering is continuous or restarts at each section or each page. You can apply the settings you make in this dialog box to the current section or to the whole document.

One other option you can set for notes is note continuation notification. In Draft view, you can open the Note pane and then enter the notice you want Word to display (for example, *Continued on next page*) when a note's text spans multiple pages.

➤ **To set options for footnotes and endnotes**

1. On the **References** tab, in the **Footnotes** group, click the dialog box launcher.

2. In the **Footnote and Endnote** dialog box, do any of the following:

   ○ In the **Location** area, select an option for positioning footnotes at the bottom of the page or below the text they refer to. For endnotes, specify whether the notes appear at the end of the document or the end of the current section.

   ○ Click **Convert** to change footnotes to endnotes, endnotes to footnotes, or to swap footnotes with endnotes (which converts both at the same time).

   ○ In the **Footnote layout** section, choose a column format or keep the default setting, which matches the column layout for the current section.

   ○ In the **Format** section, select a numbering format, insert a specific symbol for a note (such as two asterisks), specify a starting number, and select whether numbering should be continuous or should restart at each section.

   ○ In the **Apply changes to** area, select **Whole document** or **This section**.

3. Click **Insert** to add a note, or click **Apply** to apply your settings to the document.

➤ **To define a note continuation notice**

1. On the **View** tab, in the **Views** group, click **Draft**.

2. On the **References** tab, click **Show Notes**.

3. In the **Note** pane, in the list box, select **Footnote Continuation Notice** (or **Endnote Continuation Notice**).

4. In the **Note** pane, enter the text you want to use, and then close the **Note** pane.

Adding source citations to documents

To add and define bibliographic and other source citations for a document, you work with the commands in the Citations & Bibliography group on the References tab. Word provides built-in citation styles that conform to conventions defined by organizations and in traditional style manuals. For example, the style list includes entries for the American Psychological Association's style guide (APA Sixth Edition), the Modern Language Association's style guide (MLA Seventh Edition), and the sixteenth edition of the *Chicago Manual of Style*. The style option you select determines what information you enter for a citation.

You can use the Insert Citation command to add a citation that's already defined, to create a new source for a citation, or to enter a placeholder you return to later to fill in details for the source. Each citation you define is included in the gallery that appears when you click Insert Citation.

When you add a new source, you enter details in the Create Source dialog box. The fields in the Create Source dialog box depend on the bibliographic style you are using and the type of source you select. Word displays an example for each field when you select that field.

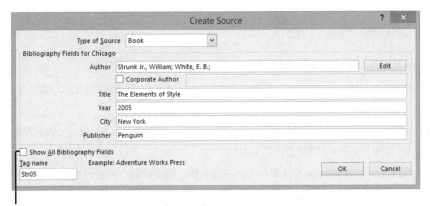

Select this check box to display a full list of
bibliographic fields, including Edition,
Translator, and Editor

To create an entry with multiple authors, click Edit beside the Author field, and then use the Edit Name dialog box to add each author name required for the citation. Word creates a tag name that identifies a particular source, using the author name you enter as the basis of the ID. You can add other information to the tag name (a year of publication, for example) to augment the information Word provides.

To make changes to a citation, click the arrow that appears on the citation's content control when you select it. The menu that appears provides options that you can use to edit the citation, edit the details for the source that is cited, convert the citation to static text, and update the citations and bibliography in the document.

In the Edit Citation dialog box, you can add page references for the citation and choose to display the author, year, and title or suppress the display of one or more of these elements.

➤ **To insert a citation**

1. On the **References** tab, in the **Citation & Bibliography** group, choose the style of citation you want to use.

2. Position the cursor where you want the citation to appear, click **Insert Citation**, and then click **Add New Source**.

3. In the **Create Source** dialog box, select the type of source, and then fill in the fields that are shown.

4. If you need to enter additional details for the source, select the **Show All Bibliography Fields** check box if you need to enter additional details for the source.

5. Click **OK**.

➤ **To use a citation placeholder**

1. Position the cursor where you want the citation to appear, click **Insert Citation**, and then click **Add New Placeholder**.

2. In the **Placeholder Name** dialog box, keep the default title provided or enter a temporary name for the source.

3. To fill in the source details, right-click the placeholder and then click **Edit Source**.

4. In the **Edit Source** dialog box, select the type of source, and then fill in the fields required.

Managing sources

When you define the details for a source in the Create Source dialog box, Word adds the reference to a master list of sources. To work with this list, you use Source Manager.

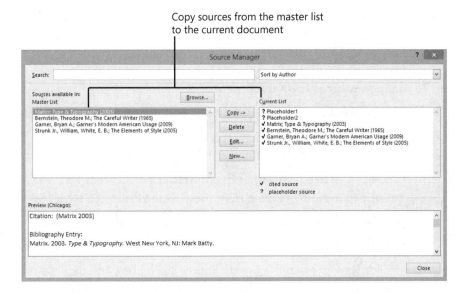

Copy sources from the master list to the current document

> **Tip** Instead of providing details for each citation as you insert them, you can build a list of sources in Source Manager. Open Source Manager, and then use the Create Source dialog box (by clicking New in Source Manager) to provide the details for each source you need to cite. Then return to the document and place citations where you need them by using the entries in the Insert Citation gallery.

Source Manager shows two lists of sources: the master list and the list for the current document. You can copy sources from the master list when you need to cite them in the current document. (You can also copy a source in the list for the current document to the master list.) Use the other command buttons in Source Manager to edit source information or to delete a source. You cannot delete a cited source (indicated by a check mark) from the current list of sources.

Word stores the sources you define in a file named Sources.xml. To view this file, click the Browse button in Source Manager to display the Open Source List dialog box. You can copy this file and use it on another computer or share it with other users. To add sources from this file to Source Manager, display the Open Source List dialog box, select Sources.xml, and then click OK. But be warned that if you have sources defined on this computer (or if another user does), that source list is replaced by those defined in the copy of Sources.xml you open.

➤ **To manage sources for a document**

1. On the **References** tab, in the **Citation & Bibliography** group, click **Manage Sources**.

2. In **Source Manager**, do any of the following:

   ○ Select a source from either the **Master List** or **Current List**, and then click **Copy** to move the source from the selected list to the target list.

   ○ Select a source, and then click **Delete** to remove it from a list.

   ○ Select a source, and then click **Edit** to update or revise details for the source.

   ○ Click **New** to open the **Create Source** dialog box and define a new source.

   ○ To change the sort order for the source lists, select an option from the **Sort** list.

   ○ To search for a particular source or set of sources, enter the search string in the **Search** box.

Inserting bibliographies

The built-in options in the Bibliography gallery include Bibliography, References, and Works Cited. Choose the option for the type of reference list you need to include in the document. The Insert Bibliography command at the bottom of the gallery adds a simply formatted bibliography to the document.

> **Tip** Bibliographies are a type of building block. You can change the formatting for the bibliography you insert, select it, and then save it to the Bibliography gallery to use in other documents. For details about working with building blocks, see section 4.1, "Create and modify building blocks."

➤ **To insert a bibliography, list of references, or list of works cited**

1. Position the cursor where you want the references to appear.

2. On the **References** tab, in the **Citation & Bibliography** group, click **Bibliography**, and then choose the option you want from the gallery that appears.

Practice tasks

The practice files for these tasks are located in the MOSWordExpert2013\
Objective3 practice file folder. Save the results of the tasks in the same folder.

- Open the *WordExpert_3-2a* document. Insert one of the built-in tables of contents from the References tab. Remove that table of contents, and then insert a custom table of contents that shows four levels of headings and includes entries formatted with the Subtitle style.

- Open the *WordExpert_3-2b* document. Create captions for the tables and figures, insert a table of figures, and then insert cross-references to several of the elements in the file.

- Open the *WordExpert_3-2c* document, and do the following:

   o Use the sources listed in the document to create a list of six or seven sources in Source Manager.

   o Open the *WordExpert_3-2d* document, and insert citations to the sources you defined in the previous task. Insert several placeholders for citations as well.

   o Open Source Manager, and edit information for three of the sources listed. Choose one or more of the entries for the placeholders you inserted, and then use the *WordExpert_3-2c* document to enter details for those placeholders.

- Insert a bibliography in the *WordExpert_3-2d* document.

3.3 Manage forms, fields, and mail merge operations

Forms are more structured than many documents you create in Word. Forms are designed to collect information in particular formats and are often submitted to other people or systems for processing or approval. Expense reports, invoices, order forms, and registration forms are examples of the types of forms you might create in Word.

When you create a form, you use content controls such as text boxes, check boxes, and lists in addition to text, images, and other document elements. You can also include fields on a form.

This section describes how to create and manage forms and how to work with fields in a document. In addition, this section describes how to set up and run a mail merge operation, a feature that relies on fields to insert information from a list of contacts.

Designing forms

You can create a form for a single document, but most forms are saved as a template so that they can be used more than once. Start with a blank template for a form you plan to design from scratch, or use one of the form templates that Word provides as a starting point.

> **See Also** For more information about templates, see section 4.2, "Create custom style sets and templates."

The information that users of a form are asked to provide can be captured in a content control such as a text box, list box, or check box. You use content controls to manage a form by specifying items for a list, for example, or by providing a defined set of options related to check boxes.

Plain text controls gather
contact information

Date-picker controls capture
arrival and departure dates

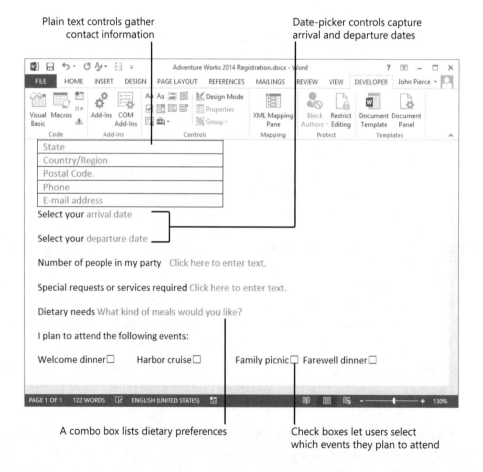

A combo box lists dietary preferences

Check boxes let users select
which events they plan to attend

The content controls you can add to a form are displayed in the Controls group on the Developer tab. (Word displays a ScreenTip that identifies each control.) When you add controls to a form, you should work in Design mode. In Design mode, Word displays the tags that identify the content controls, and you can more easily arrange and edit the content controls on the form. The following controls are available from the Controls group:

- **Rich text** Use this control for text fields in which you need to format text as bold or italic, for example, or if you need to include multiple paragraphs and add other content such as images and tables.

- **Plain text** Use the plain text control for simple text fields such as names, addresses, or job titles. The text added to a plain text control can be formatted only in limited ways, and the control can include only a single paragraph by default.

- **Combo box** In a combo box, users can select from a list of defined choices or enter their own information. If you select the Contents Cannot Be Edited property for a combo box control, users cannot add their own items to the list.

> **See Also** For more information, see the "Locking controls" topic later in this section.

- **Drop-down list** In this control, users can select only from a list of defined options. You can use a drop-down list to display department names, meeting rooms, or product names (a list of specific items). A combo box is better suited for displaying a list of tasks, for example, so that users can select a task if it appears on the list or define one if it doesn't.

- **Building block** Use a building block control when you want users of the form to choose a specific block of text or a building block from another of the galleries in Word. In a request for proposal form, for example, you might include a building block control from which users choose text entries from the Quick Parts gallery to indicate the length of time for which the proposal is valid.

> **See Also** For more information about building blocks, see section 4.1, "Create and modify building blocks."

- **Picture** Use this control to embed an image file in a document. You can use a picture control to display a logo, for example, or pictures of project personnel.

- **Date picker** This control inserts a calendar control that lets users select or enter a date.

- **Check box** Use the check box control to provide a set of options—product sizes, for example, or options that indicate which events a user plans to attend.

> **Tip** When you are designing a form, you can also work with what Word refers to as "legacy controls," which include a text box, check box, and drop-down list. For more information about working with legacy controls, see the "Working with legacy controls" topic later in this section.
>
> You can also add one of many ActiveX controls to a form. For example, you can add a command button to a form and then assign a macro to the command button. To take full advantage of ActiveX controls on a form, you should know how to program the controls with Microsoft Visual Basic for Applications (VBA). For one example of how VBA can automate controls, see the "Using macros to modify tab order in forms" topic of section 4.3, "Prepare a document for internationalization and accessibility."

Content controls include a simple text statement that tells users what to do with the control. For example, text controls display *Click here to enter text*, and the date-picker control prompts users to *Click here to enter a date*. You can customize this text so that it provides precise instructions and helps users work with a form more efficiently. Customizing the text in a control can also simplify a form.

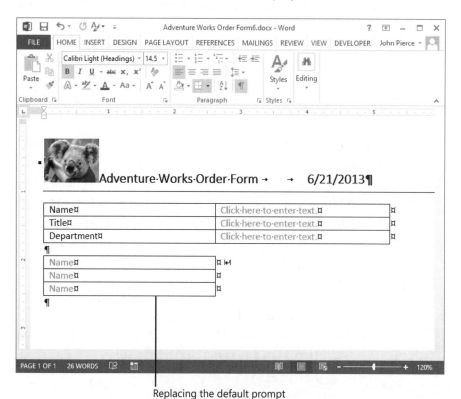

Replacing the default prompt with custom text helps simplify a form

> **Tip** To keep content controls aligned in a form, add the controls to a table. To group content controls, select the controls, and then click Group in the Controls group on the Developer tab. For example, you can group a set of check boxes so that they cannot be edited or deleted individually.

➤ **To insert a text content control**

1. Click where you want to insert the control.

2. In the **Controls** group on the **Developer** tab, click **Rich Text Content Control** or **Plain Text Content Control**.

➤ **To insert a picture control**

1. Click where you want to insert the control.

2. In the **Controls** group on the **Developer** tab, click **Picture Content Control**.

3. Click the icon in the control, and then use the **Insert Pictures** dialog box to locate and select the picture you want to display.

➤ **To insert a combo box or a drop-down list**

1. Click where you want to insert the control.

2. In the **Controls** group on the **Developer** tab, click **Combo Box Content Control** or **Drop-Down List Content Control**.

3. Select the content control, and then click **Properties** in the **Controls** group.

4. In the **Drop-Down List Properties** area, click **Add**, and then use the **Add Choice** dialog box to define the first item for the list. Repeat this step to define each item required in the list.

5. Select options for other properties, and then click **OK**.

➤ **To insert a date picker**

1. Click where you want to insert the date picker control.

2. In the **Controls** group on the **Developer** tab, click **Date Picker Content Control**.

➤ **To insert a check box**

1. Click where you want to insert the check box control.

2. In the **Controls** group on the **Developer** tab, click **Check Box Content Control**.

➤ **To insert a building block**

1. Click where you want to insert the control.

2. In the **Controls** group on the **Developer** tab, click **Building Block Gallery Content Control**.

3. Click the content control to select it, and then click **Properties** in the **Controls** group.

4. Click the gallery and the category for the building blocks that you want to make available in the building block control, and then click **OK**.

➤ **To customize the text in a content control**

1. In the **Controls** group, click **Design Mode**.

2. Select the content control you want to edit.

3. Edit the placeholder text, and apply any formatting.

4. In the **Controls** group, click **Design Mode** to exit Design mode.

Working with control properties

Each control you add to a form has a set of properties. The most basic properties are Title and Tag. Properties also affect how the contents of a control are formatted, whether the control can be deleted, and whether its content can be edited. Other properties depend on the type of control you are working with. For example, for a plain text control, you can set an option to allow multiple paragraphs. Properties for the date-picker control include the date format, the locale, and the calendar type.

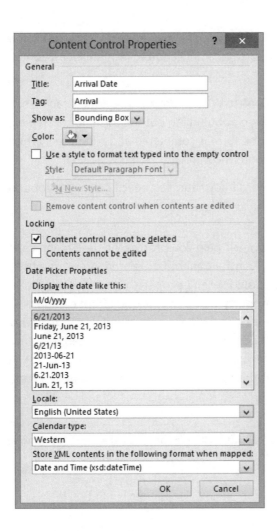

Word displays a control's title to identify it. The Tag property helps you locate a control and can be used if you link your form to a data source. Tags enclose a control when you work in Design mode.

The property Remove Content Control When Contents Are Edited can be set when you use a control to provide information about filling out the form, for example, but the content control is not needed when the form is completed and submitted. (This property is not available for the check box content control.)

The following sections provide more information on specific control properties.

Locking controls

Two properties you can set for controls help you protect the design and content of your form. The first property, Content Control Cannot Be Deleted, prevents a user of a form from deleting that control. You should set this property on every control that is required in the form. You can also set a property that prevents users from editing the content of a control. This property is suitable for titles, for example, or other controls whose content should remain static, such as text controls that display standardized text. Many controls, however, require users to enter text, choose an option, or select from a list. For controls such as these, you should not set the option to prevent the content of a control from being edited.

> **See Also** For more information about locking a form, see the topic "Locking and unlocking forms" later in this section.

Formatting controls

In the Content Control Properties dialog box, by selecting Use A Style To Format Text Typed Into The Empty Control, you can apply a style to the content in a control. You can choose a style from the Style list or create a style in the Create New Style From Formatting dialog box.

> **See Also** For information about creating styles, see section 2.2, "Apply advanced styles."

Building lists

If you are using a combo box or list box content control, the Content Control Properties dialog box includes fields that you use to define list items. In the dialog box, you specify the display name and value for each list item.

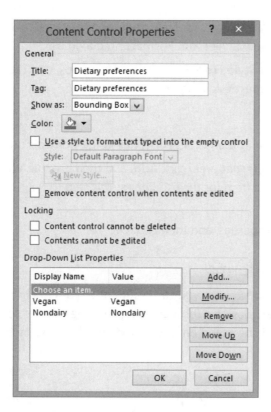

By default, Word repeats the text you enter in the Display Name box in the Value box (or vice versa, if you enter a value first). You can change the value to a numerical value, for example, to match a sequence of choices.

➤ **To lock a control**

1. Select the content control, and then click **Properties** in the **Controls** group.

2. In the **Content Control Properties** dialog box, in the **Locking** area, select one or both of the options that apply:

   ○ **Content control cannot be deleted**

   ○ **Contents cannot be edited**

3. Click **OK**.

➤ **To format a control**

1. Select the content control, and then click **Properties** in the **Controls** group.

2. In the **Content Control Properties** dialog box, select the **Use a style to format text typed into the empty control** check box.

3. Choose a style from the **Style** list, or click **New Style**, and then define the attributes of the style in the **Create New Style From Formatting** dialog box.

4. Click **OK** in the **Create New Style From Formatting** dialog box, and then click **OK** in the **Content Control Properties** dialog box.

➤ **To define a list**

1. Select the content control, and then click **Properties** in the **Controls** group.

2. In the **Drop-Down List Properties** area, click **Add**, and then use the **Add Choice** dialog box to define the first item for the list. Repeat this step to define each item required in the list.

3. Select options for other properties, and then click **OK**.

Locking and unlocking forms

As you can with other types of documents, you can restrict the types of changes users can make to a form. After you design a form and set properties for the controls it contains, use the Restrict Editing command on the Developer tab to display the Restrict Editing pane.

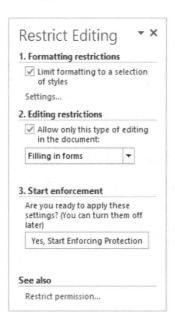

Select the option to limit formatting if you want to maintain the look and feel of the form. The Filling In Forms option in the Editing Restrictions list sets up the form so that users can edit controls as you designated, but they cannot change the design of the form or alter the text in titles or other labels.

> **Important** The Filling In Forms option does not let you specify groups or individuals who can make changes to the document. It controls only how users can work with the form. For more information on restricting editing to groups or individuals, see the "Restricting editing" topic in section 1.2, "Prepare documents for review."

When a user bases a new document on a form template you've designed, he or she can fill in the required fields but cannot perform other types of edits. If a user clicks Restrict Editing, the pane that Word displays describes this situation and presents the user with a Stop Protection button. To unlock the form and make changes other than filling in the form's fields, a user must click Stop Protection and then provide a password if a password is assigned to restrict the editing of the form.

> **Tip** To specify users who can bypass editing restrictions and work with the form while protection is applied, click Restrict Permission at the bottom of the Restrict Editing pane. In the Select User dialog box, select the user accounts to which you want to grant this privilege.

➤ To lock a form

1. On the **Developer** tab, in the **Protect** group, click **Restrict Editing**.

2. In the **Restrict Editing** pane, select the **Allow only this type of editing in the document** check box in the **Editing Restrictions** area, and then choose **Filling in Forms** from the list.

3. Click **Yes, Start Enforcing Protection**.

4. In the **Start Enforcing Protection** dialog box, enter a password, and then enter the password again to confirm it.

5. Click **OK** in the **Start Enforcing Protection** dialog box.

Working with legacy controls

In Word, you can work with three legacy controls, which are also referred to as *form fields*: a text box, a check box, and a drop-down list. You can add these fields to a form in addition to content controls and then set options for how users can interact and work with the fields. For each form field, Word provides an Options dialog box in which you can specify settings for how the form field behaves. (Double-click the field to display the dialog box.)

The following settings are available:

- **Text box** In the Text Form FieldType list, you can choose the type of data the text field will contain (options include Regular Text, Number, and Date). The Type list also includes Calculation, which lets you define an expression that is evaluated when a user works with the form field.

  Use the Default Text box to define the text (or number or date) you want the field to show by default. In the Maximum Length box, Unlimited is the default option, but you can specify a certain number of characters. For example, a product ID might include exactly nine characters, and you can specify that in the Maximum Length box. The Text Format list changes depending on the choice you make in the Type list. Currency formatting options, for example, are available when you select Number in the Type list.

  Use the Run Macro On lists to select a macro that you want Word to run when a user enters or exits the field. Leave the Fill-In Enabled check box selected if you want users to be able to edit the contents of the field. Select Calculate On Exit if the form field is set up to calculate an expression.

- **Check box** For a check box form field, you can specify its size and whether it is selected or not selected by default. As you can with a text form field, you can specify a macro that runs when a user enters or exits the field.

- **Drop-down list** Use the Options dialog box for a drop-down list form field to define the items for the list. In the Run Macro On lists, choose a macro if you want to run one when a user enters or exits this field.

The Options dialog box for each type of form field includes the Add Help Text button. The Form Field Help Text dialog box contains two pages: Status Bar and Help Key (F1). You can select AutoText Entry and then choose an item from the list provided by Word, or select Type Your Own and then enter the help text you want to display to users on the status bar or in the Help window when a user presses F1.

Form fields do not become active unless you follow the steps outlined in the previous section ("Locking and unlocking a form") to apply editing restrictions for the form. When editing restrictions are enforced, you cannot change the properties of a form field. You must stop protection (by entering the specified password) before you can make any adjustments.

To remove a form field, remove protection from the form if necessary, select the field, and then press Delete.

➤ **To build a form by using form fields**

1. Click where you want to insert the field.

2. On the **Developer** tab, in the **Controls** group, click **Legacy Tools**, and then select the type of form field you want to add (text, check box, or drop-down list).

3. Double-click the field placeholder in the form to open the selected form field's **Options** dialog box.

4. In the **Form Field Options** dialog box, set properties for the form field (for example, define the list items for a drop-down list form field, or specify the default value for a text form field).

5. Click **Add Help Text**, and then define the help text you want to appear on the status bar and in the Help window.

6. After you finish adding form fields and defining each field's properties, click **Restrict Editing** on the **Developer** tab.

7. In the **Restrict Editing** pane, select the check box under **Editing Restrictions**, and then select **Filling in forms** from the list.

8. Click **Yes, Start Enforcing Protection**, and then enter the password you want to use to protect this form.

> **To remove a form field**

1. With the form open, click **Restrict Editing** on the **Developer** tab.

2. In the **Restrict Editing** pane, click **Stop Protection**.

3. In the **Unprotect Document** dialog box, enter the password used to protect the form, and then click **OK**.

4. Select the form field you want to remove, and then press **Delete**.

Inserting and managing document fields

As described earlier in this chapter, Word uses fields to manage elements such as indexes, tables of contents, and tables of authorities. You can also insert fields on your own to display information automatically. When the information that a field displays changes, you can update the field so it's current. (To update a field, select it and then press F9.)

> **See Also** For details about formatting fields, see section 2.1, "Apply advanced formatting."

The Field dialog box lists fields in categories such as Date And Time, Document Automation, Document Information, Links And References, and User Information. You can display all fields or only the fields in a particular category. (Document properties such as Author, Keywords, and Title are listed in the Document Information category.)

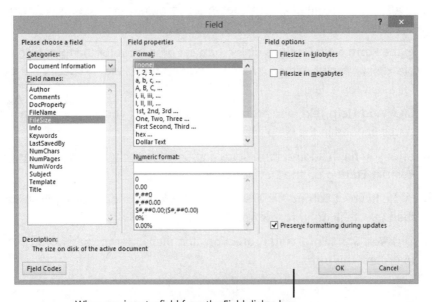

When you insert a field from the Field dialog box,
use the field's description and the lists of properties
and options Word provides to set up the field

You can view the output of the field or the field code itself. The field code includes the field's name (such as *FileSize*) and can also include properties and other switches that affect how the field's data is formatted and what the field displays. For example, the field code *{FILESIZE * CardNumber \k * MERGEFORMAT}* shows a document's file size as a cardinal number in kilobytes. The *MERGEFORMAT* switch indicates that the field's format remains the same when it is updated.

Word provides keyboard shortcuts you can use to manage fields in a document, as shown in the following table.

Keyboard shortcut	Action
Ctrl+F9	Inserts a blank field
Alt+F9	Switches the view between field codes and field output for all fields in the document
Shift+F9	Switches the view between field codes and field output for selected fields
F9	Updates selected fields
F11 or Shift+F11	Moves to the next or previous field
Ctrl+F11	Locks a field and prevents it from being updated
Ctrl+Shift+F11	Unlocks a field

> **See Also** For a reference of field properties and options, see the Word Help system topic "Field codes in Word."

> **To insert a field**

1. On the **Insert** tab, in the **Text** group, click **Quick Parts**, and then click **Field**.

2. In the **Field** dialog box, select the field you want to insert. Use the **Categories** list to view a subset of the fields.

3. In the **Field properties** area, select properties for formatting.

4. In the **Field options** area, select the options you want to use with the field.

5. To view the elements of the field code, click **Field Codes**.

6. Click **Options** to open the **Field Options** dialog box, and then select the switches you want to apply.

Performing mail merge operations

Viewing the results of a successful mail merge operation can be very satisfying. After some preliminary work on your part—creating the document you want to send and identifying information about the document's recipients—Word takes over, merges the content and information you supply, and produces each document you need. You can incorporate additional options to control how Word produces the documents, and you aren't limited to producing paper mailings—you can send a personal email message to each recipient in a group by using the mail merge features in Word.

Setting up and running a mail merge operation entails six steps (roughly moving left to right across the Mailings tab on the ribbon):

1. Open the document you want to use in the mail merge operation, or start with a blank document and add text, illustrations, and other content. You can enter the content of the document later in the process, but you must have at least a blank document open to enable the commands you need on the Mailings tab.

2. Click Start Mail Merge to display options for the type of mail merge operation you can run—Letters, E-Mail Messages, Envelopes, Labels, Directory, or Normal Word Document.

> **Tip** A directory is like a catalog. It includes the same type of information about a group of items (for example, the name of each item, a description, and a price), but the information is distinct for each item.

3. Click Select Recipients, and then choose an option for the source of your recipient list. You can use the Edit Recipient List command to display the recipient list to select a subset from the list or to update information. In the dialog box Word displays, you can sort and filter the list to organize and find particular entries.

4. Use the commands in the Write & Insert Fields group to insert an address block, a greeting line, and other merge fields, which are placeholders that Word uses to display information contained in the recipient list when you run the mail merge operation.

5. Preview the results. You can find a particular recipient or move from record to record in the list. Word can also check for errors in advance and compile those errors in a separate document.

6. Click Finish & Merge. You can edit and save individual documents, print the documents all at once, or send the document as an email message.

> **Tip** The last option listed on the Start Mail Merge menu is Step By Step Mail Merge Wizard. The wizard opens a pane that leads you through the six mail merge steps.

Building and managing recipient lists

Names, addresses, and other information you want to include about recipients in your mail merge documents can come from a variety of sources. You can create an address list as a step in a mail merge operation or use a list that's stored in a Microsoft Excel worksheet, a Microsoft Access database, your contacts list in Microsoft Outlook, or one of several other formats.

> **Tip** To be of best use in a mail merge, the information in an external data source should be organized as you need to use it for recipient information. For example, if you are compiling an address list in Excel, it's best to include a header row with column names that correspond to the fields Word uses for addresses in a mail merge operation.

The Type A New List option on the Select Recipients menu opens the New Address List dialog box, where you can compile a recipient list for the mail merge operation. After you build the list, Word saves it in .mdb format. You can select this list for other mail merge operations in the future.

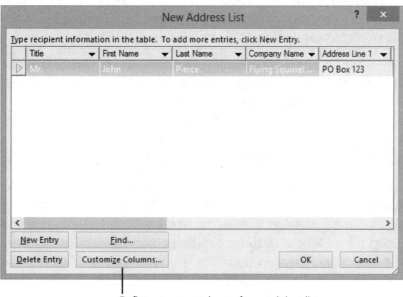

Define your own columns for a recipient list
by clicking Customize Columns

Scroll to the right in this dialog box to view the group of fields available by default. You can use the Customize Columns button to open a dialog box in which you can define additional fields, delete fields you don't need, rename fields, and change the order in which the fields appear. By defining a custom field, you expand the type of information you can insert and display in a mail merge operation. For example, you could create a field named Donation and enter the amount a recipient donated to your organization, or you could create a field named Auction Item and use it to describe what someone purchased at an auction. The amount of information you can store in a custom field is limited to 254 characters, including spaces.

In the New Address List dialog box, click a column heading to sort the list by that column, or click the arrow beside a column heading to open a menu to sort and filter the list in other ways. You can filter for a particular value, filter for blank values to fill in missing information, or use the Advanced option to open the Filter And Sort dialog box. On the Sort Records page in the Filter And Sort dialog box, you can specify as many as three fields to sort by. On the Filter Records page, you can set up a simple, single-field filter to find all records that equal (or do not equal) a particular value, for example, or you can define multifield filters by using the OR and AND operators. Use the OR operator when you want to view records that match any of the conditions you define. Use the AND operator to select records that match each condition you define.

The Comparison list on the Filter Records page includes the Less Than, Greater Than, Less Than Or Equal, Greater Than Or Equal, and other operators. You can use these operators to find records with specific numeric values in a custom field you create. For example, for a mail merge operation related to a fundraising campaign, you could create and populate a custom field named Pledge or Donation and then filter on the values for that field (pledges above $1,000, for example) to send a document only to those recipients.

If you select an Excel workbook or an Access database as the source of a recipient list, Word displays the Select Table dialog box. This dialog box lists each worksheet and named range in an Excel workbook or the tables and queries defined in an Access database. Select the worksheet, range, or database object you want to use. The First Row Of Data Contains Column Headers check box is selected by default. Clear this check box if the data source you select isn't set up that way.

A Word document that contains nothing but a table is also a valid source of data for a recipient list. Set up a table with the column headings you want to use for fields in the mail merge, enter the recipient data in table rows, and then save the table as a separate document.

If the information you want to use for the recipient list is stored in a server database (for example, a Microsoft SQL Server database), you can use the Data Connection wizard to create a connection. As you step through the wizard, you need to provide information such as the server name and the user name and password required to gain access to the server. Choosing the Other/Advanced option in the wizard leads you to the Data Link Properties dialog box. In this dialog box, you select a data source provider and specify the information and other initialization properties required to make a connection. You might need to obtain some of this information from a network or server administrator. Use the Help button in the Data Link Properties dialog box to obtain detailed information about each field.

If you maintain and manage a detailed contacts list in Outlook—including information such as company names, phone numbers, mailing addresses, and other details—you can make productive use of your contacts folder as the data source for a mail merge operation. All the contacts in the folder you choose are selected for the operation by default. Clear the check box beside any contact that you don't want to correspond with in the mail merge operation you are setting up.

> **Tip** If you make changes to your Outlook contact list, click Refresh to update the list of recipients for the mail merge. Keep in mind that you cannot edit Outlook contact information while working in the Mail Merge Recipients dialog box.

➤ **To create and manage an address list**

1. On the **Mailings** tab, click **Select Recipients**, and then click **Type New List**.

2. In the **New Address List** dialog box, enter the information for the first recipient and then click **New Entry**.

3. Repeat step 2 to add all the recipients you need in this list.

4. To delete an entry, select the row, and then click **Delete Entry**.

5. To locate a specific recipient in the list, click **Find**. In the **Find Entry** dialog box, enter the text string you want Word to find. This might be a first name, a last name, a city name, or a value related to a different field. To search for this text in a specific field, click **This Field** and then choose the field you want to search. Click **Find Next**. Click **Cancel** when you locate the field you are looking for.

6. In the **New Address List** dialog box, click **OK**.

7. In the **Save Address List** dialog box, open the folder where you want to save this address list, and then click **Save**.

➤ **To customize an address list**

1. In the **New Address List** dialog box, click **Customize Columns**.

2. Do one or more of the following:

   ○ To add a custom field, click **Add,** enter the name of the field in the **Add Field** dialog box, and then click **OK**.

   ○ To change the order of the fields, select the field you want to move and then click **Move Up** or **Move Down**.

➤ **To select an external data source**

1. In the **Start Mail Merge** group, click **Select Recipients**, and then click **Use Existing List**.

2. In the **Select Data Source** dialog box, open the folder that contains the data source file you want to use.

3. If the type of file you need isn't displayed, in the **Files Of Type** list, select that file format.

4. Select the data source file, and then click **Open**.

5. Depending on the type of data source you select, use the **Select Table** dialog box to choose the worksheet, cell range, or database object that contains the recipient information you want.

➤ **To use an Outlook contact folder as a recipient list**

1. In the **Start Mail Merge** group, click **Select Recipients**, and then click **Choose From Outlook Contacts**.

2. If prompted, choose the Outlook profile that is associated with the contacts folder you want to use.

3. In the **Select Contacts** dialog box, select the contacts folder, and then click **OK**.

4. In the **Mail Merge Recipients** dialog box, clear the check box beside the name of any contact you don't want to include in this mail merge.

5. To refresh the list so that it shows recent changes made in Outlook, select **Contacts** in the **Data Source** area and then click **Refresh**.

Modifying recipient lists

When you click Edit Recipient List in the Start Mail Merge group, Word displays the Mail Merge Recipients dialog box. To exclude a recipient from a mail merge operation, clear the check box beside the recipient's name.

Use the arrows beside a column name to sort or filter the list, or use the links listed in the Refine Recipient List area. For example, you might want to sort by city or by company for a mailing you are preparing for contacts at particular clients or in particular locales.

The Sort and Filter commands in the Refine Recipient List area open the Filter And Sort dialog box. (You can also open this dialog box by choosing Advanced from the menu that appears when you click the arrow next to a column heading.)

> **See Also** For more information about using the Filter And Sort dialog box, see the "Building and managing recipient lists" topic earlier in this section.

The Find Duplicates command displays a dialog box that lists what Word determines are duplicate entries. Clear the check box for entries you don't want to include. You can also locate a specific contact by searching in all fields or specific fields for values such as last name or company name.

For certain types of data sources (Excel workbooks and Access databases, for example, but not for Outlook contact lists), you can edit detailed information about recipients.

➤ **To edit a recipient list**

1. In the **Start Mail Merge** group, click **Edit Recipient List**.

2. In the **Mail Merge Recipients** dialog box, select the recipient list in the **Data Source** area, and then click **Edit**.

3. In the **Edit Data Source** dialog box, update the values for fields, or click **New Entry** to add a recipient record.

4. In the **Edit Data Source** dialog box, click **OK**. In the message box Word displays, click **Yes** to update the recipient list and save the changes to the original data source.

➤ **To refine a recipient list**

1. In the **Start Mail Merge** group, click **Edit Recipient List**. In the **Mail Merge Recipients** dialog box, do any of the following:

   ○ Use the arrows beside column headings to sort the list by that field (in ascending or descending order) or to filter the list by values in that field or for blank or nonblank fields.

   ○ For more advanced sorts, in the **Refine Recipient List** area, click **Sort** to open the **Filter and Sort** dialog box. On the **Sort Records** tab, you can sort by up to three fields.

○ To define an advanced filter, in the **Refine Recipient List** area, click **Filter**. On the **Filter Records** page of the **Filter and Sort** dialog box, select the field you want to filter by. Select a comparison operator, and then enter the text you want to use for the filter. In the far left column, you can also select the **AND** or **OR** operator and then add another field to the filter. Repeat this step to define other conditions for the filter.

○ To check for duplicate recipients, click **Find Duplicates**. In the **Find Duplicates** dialog box, clear the check box beside the duplicate entries you don't want to include.

○ To locate a specific recipient, click **Find Recipient**. In the **Find Entry** dialog box, enter the text you want Word to search for. To search in a particular field, select **This Field**, and then select the field you want to use.

2. In the **Mail Merge Recipients** dialog box, click **OK**.

Adding merge fields

Merge fields correspond to the columns of information in a recipient list. To add the information stored in a recipient list to a document, you insert merge fields where you want the information to appear. You can place the information at the start of the document to define an address block or a greeting and also within the body of the document, where you might include a company name, for example, or other information.

Word provides composite merge fields for an address block and a greeting line. The Address Block command in the Write & Insert Fields group inserts standard information such as title, first and last names, mailing address, city, state, country/region, and postal code. In the Insert Address Block dialog box, you can tailor the address block so that it fits the needs of the mail merge operation you have underway.

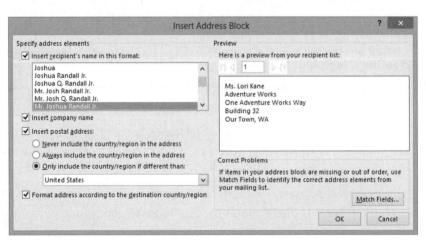

The ways you can modify the standard address block include the following:

- Choose a format for recipient names (first name only, first and last names, first and last names with title, and others).

- Clear the check box for the Insert Company Name option if you don't want to include that information. (The check box is selected by default.)

- Clear the check box for Insert Postal Address. For example, you might want only names to appear in the document and use address information for labels or envelopes. You can also specify under what conditions you want the country/region name to appear in the address block.

The Greeting Line command presents similar kinds of options. You can alter the salutation from Dear to To, for example, and specify how recipient names appear. Use the Greeting Line For Invalid Recipient Names list to choose a greeting that Word applies when information in the recipient list doesn't match the format you choose for a name.

To insert individual merge fields, including any custom fields you define when building a recipient list, choose the fields from the Insert Merge Field list or use the Insert Merge Field dialog box. In the dialog box, select the Address Fields option to display an extended list of fields.

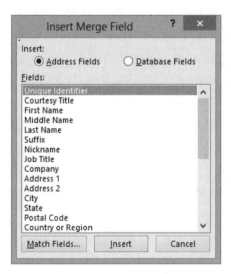

You can insert these fields at any place in the document that makes sense. For example, in the final paragraph of a letter, you might repeat the recipient's first name for emphasis—"In closing, I want to thank you again, <<*First_Name*>>, for your support of Adventure Works."

If the fields in an Excel worksheet or other data source you are using for recipient information don't correspond one-to-one with the fields in Word, use the Match Fields command in the Write & Insert Fields group to open a dialog box in which you can set up the field relationships you need. (You can also open this dialog box by clicking the Match Fields button in the Insert Address Block or Insert Greeting Line dialog box.)

If a field in your data source doesn't match a field in Word, Word displays Not Matched. To match the fields in Word (listed at the left), select a field from the list to its right. Keep in mind that you cannot include any unmatched fields in the mail merge document. You can save the configuration of matching fields if you expect to use this data source for other mail merge operations on the computer you are using.

> **Tip** You don't need to complete a mail merge operation in one sitting. You can save a document you are preparing for a mail merge operation, and Word maintains the association with the data source for recipients and any merge fields you have inserted. When you open the document to begin work again, click Yes in the message box that Word displays to confirm that you want to open the document and run an SQL command.

➤ **To insert an address block**

1. In the document, place the cursor where you want the address block to appear.

2. In the **Write & Insert Fields** group, click **Address Block**.

3. In the **Insert Address Block** dialog box, do any of the following:

   ○ Choose a format for recipient names, or clear the **Insert Recipient's Name In This Format** option to exclude names from the address block.

   ○ Specify whether you want to include a company name and postal address.

   ○ Select an option for when to include the country/region name in the address block.

   ○ Specify whether to format the address block using conventions for the destination country or region.

4. Use the **Preview** area to check how your choices affect the display of addresses.

➤ **To insert a greeting line**

1. In the document, place the cursor where you want the greeting line to appear.

2. In the **Write & Insert Fields** group, click **Greeting Line**.

3. In the **Insert Greeting Line** dialog box, do any of the following:

   ○ Specify a format for the elements of the greeting line, including the salutation and name format.

   ○ Choose a format for invalid recipient names.

4. Use the **Preview** area to view how your choices affect how the greeting line will appear.

➤ **To insert a merge field**

1. In the document, place the cursor where you want the merge field to appear.

2. In the **Write & Insert Fields** group, click **Insert Merge Field,** and then select the field you want to use, or open the **Insert Merge Field** dialog box, select the field, and then click **Insert**.

➤ **To match fields**

1. In the **Write and Insert Fields** group, click **Match Fields**.

2. In the **Match Fields** dialog box, match the field names Word provides with field names in your recipient list.

3. Click **OK**.

Using mail merge rules

Mail merge rules enable you to define conditional elements that can add flexibility and help customize records produced in a mail merge operation. The rules are listed on the Rules menu in the Write & Insert Fields group.

One helpful rule is the If Then Else rule. In the dialog box you use to set up this rule, you first specify an IF condition (for example, "If the Country field is equal to Canada"). In the Insert This Text box, enter the text you want Word to insert when the condition you define is true. In the Otherwise Insert This Text box, enter the text you want Word to insert when the IF condition is false.

Set up mail merge rules to
customize content on the
basis of conditions you define

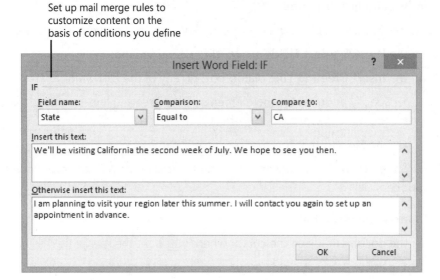

Two other rules you might make use of are Ask and Fill In. These rules can prompt you as each mail merge document is produced so that you can change information on the fly. To set up an Ask rule, position the cursor where you want to insert specific text, and then click Ask on the Rules menu. In the Insert Word Field: Ask dialog box, enter a name for a bookmark. For example, create a bookmark named Discount where you want to specify the discount that a customer is going to receive. In the Prompt box, enter a prompt that lets you or another user know what text to enter. In the Default Bookmark Text box, enter the text you want to appear by default.

Select the Ask Once check box if you want to be prompted only at the start of the final mail merge. Keep the check box clear if you want the prompt to appear for each record. After you close the dialog box, Word displays only a marker indicating that you've inserted the bookmark.

Now switch to the Insert tab on the ribbon, click Quick Parts, and then click Field. In the Field dialog box, scroll down in the Field Names list and select the Ref field. In the Field Properties area of the dialog box, select the name of the bookmark you created. Close the Field dialog box, and the default text now appears in the document. When you start merging documents, you'll be prompted to accept the default text or insert an alternative for the particular document then being produced.

The Fill-In rule works similarly. Position your cursor where you want to be prompted to fill in certain information. Click Fill-In on the Rules menu, and then enter a prompt and default text in the Insert Word Field: Fill-In dialog box.

To associate a specific value with a bookmark, use the Set Bookmark rule. In the dialog box Word displays, enter a name for the bookmark and then enter the value you want to associate with the bookmark. You can place the bookmark in multiple locations in the document (wherever the value you associate with it needs to appear). If you need to update the value later, you can edit the field's value once rather than update every instance.

➤ **To define an If Then Else merge rule**

1. In the **Write & Insert Fields** group, click **Rules**, and then click **If Then Else**.

2. In the **Insert Word Field: If** dialog box, select the field you want to use in an IF condition, select a comparison operator, and then enter the text or other value you want to match.

3. In the **Insert This Text** box, enter the text that you want Word to insert when the IF condition is true.

4. In the **Otherwise Insert This Text** box, enter the text that should appear when the condition you define is false.

Previewing mail merge results

On the Mailings tab, click Preview Results to display merge fields so that they show recipient records. Use the Find Recipient command to locate a specific recipient, or use the preview arrows to move from record to record in the recipient list.

Word can check for errors before you print documents or run your mail merge via email. The dialog box that Word displays provides three options: simulating the merge and reporting errors in a new document, running the merge and pausing if Word encounters an error, and completing the merge and reporting errors in a separate document. The types of errors Word checks for include missing information in the recipient list.

Sending personal email messages to groups of recipients

As long as you have a compatible email program (Outlook, for example), you can set up a mail merge operation to send an email message to a list of recipients. Each message is a single item addressed to a single recipient—the message isn't sent to the group as a whole—and you can personalize each message as you might a mail merge document by using, for example, only a first name.

One key in sending email messages is that your data source should include a column labeled E-Mail Address in the header row. Set up the document with an address block, greeting line, and other merge fields as you would for a printed letter. You can then preview the results of each message you plan to send.

In the Merge To E-Mail dialog box, select the field you want to use for the message's To line (most likely, E-Mail Address), enter a subject line, and then select a format for the message (Attachment, HTML, or Plain Text). In the Send Records area of the dialog box, you can specify whether to send the message to all recipients, the current recipient, or a subset of recipient records.

➤ **To send a personal email message as a mail merge document**

1. Create the document you want to send as an email message.

2. Select or build the recipient list, insert merge fields, and define merge rules as necessary.

3. On the **Mailings** tab, in the **Finish** group, click **Finish & Merge**, and then click **Send Email Messages**.

4. In the **Merge to E-mail** dialog box, select the field to use for the message's **To** line.

5. Enter a subject line for the message, and then select a message format.

6. Select which recipient records you want to send the message to, and then click **OK**.

Setting up labels or envelopes for mail merge operations

The Mailings tab provides a couple of ways to create and print labels and envelopes. You can use the Envelopes or Labels option on the Start Mail Merge menu to merge information from your recipient list to produce the envelopes or labels you need. You can use the Envelopes and Labels commands in the Create group (at the far left of the Mailings tab) to prepare and print these items without setting up a full mail merge operation.

When you are preparing to print labels or envelopes as part of a mail merge operation, start with a blank document. If you have a document open when you select either option from the Start Mail Merge menu and then click OK in the Envelope Options or Label Options dialog box, Word displays a warning telling you that it must delete the contents of the open document and discard any changes before it can continue.

Depending on the options you select for envelopes or labels (envelope size, for example, or label vendor and product number), Word displays a document with an area in which you insert merge fields. Enter or select a recipient list, and then add the merge fields you want to include on the envelope or labels. You can use the Address Block command, for example, or add individual merge fields. You can also add merge rules. For example, you might add the Merge Record # rule as a way to determine how many labels or envelopes you print.

With merge fields in place, you can preview the results and then use the Finish & Merge menu to print the labels or envelopes.

➤ **To set up envelopes for mail merge**

1. Create a blank document.
2. On the **Start Mail Merge** menu, click **Envelopes**.
3. In the **Envelope Options** dialog box, select the envelope size.
4. Change the font formatting for the addresses as needed.
5. On the **Printing Options** tab, check that the settings are correct for the printer you are using.
6. Click **OK**.
7. Click **Select Recipients**, and then choose an option for the recipient list you want to use.
8. Add merge fields to the envelope to create an address block.
9. Preview the results, and check for any errors.
10. Click **Finish & Merge**, and then click **Print Documents**.

➤ **To set up labels for mail merge**

1. Create a blank document.
2. On the **Start Mail Merge** menu, click **Labels**.
3. In the **Label Options** dialog box, select the type of printer you are using.
4. In the **Label Information** area, select the label vendor and then the product number for the label you are using.
5. Click **OK**.
6. Click **Select Recipients**, and then choose an option for the recipient list you want to use.
7. Add merge fields to the document to create an address block.
8. Preview the results, and check for any errors.
9. Click **Finish & Merge**, and then click **Print Documents**.

Practice tasks

The practice files for these tasks are located in the MOSWordExpert2013\ Objective3 practice file folder. Save the results of the tasks in the same folder.

- Open the *WordExpert_3-3a* document, and do the following:

  ○ Using the content controls available in Word 2013, add the content controls referred to in the document and set the properties for the content controls as specified. This practice task will result in an order form in which users select products, specify the quantity and color they want for each item, and then specify selection options for shipping, along with special instructions, if needed. When you are finished, save the form using the name *Order form*.

  ○ Add a form field of each type to the form you created in the previous task (*Order form*).

  ○ Protect the *Order form* document by using the Restrict Editing command. Remove protection, and then delete one or more of the form fields you added in the previous step.

- Open a new blank document. Select the *WordExpert_3-3b* workbook to use as the recipient list, and then print a practice sheet of labels for a mail merge operation. You can experiment with different label sizes.

- Open the *WordExpert_3-3c* document, then do the following:

  ○ Choose the option to use an existing list as the recipient list. Select the *WordExpert_3-3b* workbook.

  ○ Use the Match Fields command so that the merge fields for addresses in Word match fields listed in the *WordExpert_3-3b* workbook.

  ○ Edit the recipient list by adding an entry of your own and changing the values in some of the fields.

- Open the *WordExpert_3-3d* document, and then do the following:

  ○ Choose the option to create an email message mail merge operation.

  ○ Using the list of names on page 2 of the *WordExpert_3-3d*, create an address list in Word. Also, create a custom address list field named Position.

  ○ Edit the recipient list, adding a contact of your own. Add your email address to the E-Mail Address field for a handful of recipients.

> - Insert an address block, and then insert the Position field in the high-lighted area of the document.
>
> - Create an If Then Else merge rule for the Position field that inserts the text "I am interested in your writer position" for the records in which Position equals Writer. For other records, use the text "I am interested in your recently announced position."
>
> - Preview records, and then run the email merge operation.

Objective review

Before finishing this chapter, ensure that you have mastered the following skills:

3.1 Create and manage indexes

3.2 Create and manage reference tables

3.3 Manage forms, fields, and mail merge operations

4 Create custom Word elements

The skills tested in this section of the Microsoft Office Specialist Expert exams for Microsoft Word 2013 relate to creating custom Word elements, including building blocks and style sets. Specifically, the following objectives are associated with this set of skills:

4.1 Create and modify building blocks

4.2 Create custom style sets and templates

4.3 Prepare a document for internationalization and accessibility

This chapter guides you in studying ways to customize features you use to build and design Word documents. The chapter first describes how to create and modify building blocks, such as cover pages and headers or footers. It then covers how to work with custom style sets, templates, and theme colors and fonts. The chapter's final section outlines steps you can take to make documents accessible—for example, by including alternative text that screen readers use to describe images and illustrations—and how to implement content standards for international audiences.

> **Practice Files** To complete the practice tasks in this chapter, you need the practice files contained in the MOSWordExpert2013\Objective4 practice file folder. For more information, see "Download the practice files" in this book's Introduction.

4.1 Create and modify building blocks

Galleries in Word 2013 are filled with what are known as *building blocks*. Word provides building blocks for headers and footers, cover pages, tables, and other document elements. Word displays a list of building blocks in the Building Blocks Organizer, a dialog box you can open by clicking Quick Parts on the Insert tab and then clicking Building Blocks Organizer. Select a building block in the list to display a preview and a description.

Click a column heading to sort
the list of building blocks

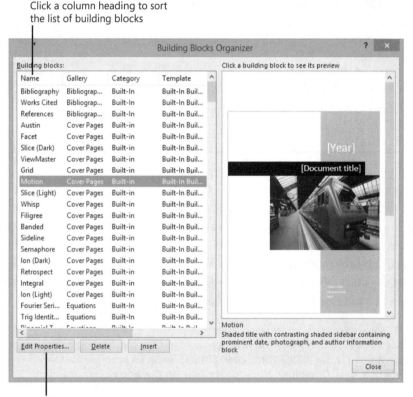

Click Edit Properties to change the gallery
or category for a building block

Editing building block properties

Each building block is defined by a set of properties that you can use to keep building blocks organized and to specify how Word inserts the building block. In the Modify Building Block dialog box (click Edit Properties in the Building Blocks Organizer to open this dialog box), you can change the gallery a building block is assigned to, its category, its description, and other properties.

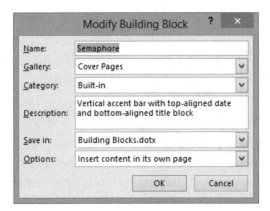

In the Modify Building Block dialog box, you can set or change the following properties:

- **Name** The name of the building block.

- **Gallery** The gallery in which you want the building block to appear. Use the built-in galleries (such as AutoText or Cover Page) or one of the galleries Word provides named *Custom*. You cannot enter your own gallery name.

- **Category** You can assign a building block to a category within a gallery. Items in a gallery are grouped by their category. Click Create New Category in this list to define a custom category.

- **Description** This section provides the description that appears in a ScreenTip when you point to the building block in a gallery and when you select the item in the Building Blocks Organizer.

- **Save in** This box specifies the template in which to save the building block. The options you can choose from include Normal.dotm (the default Word template), Building Blocks.dotx (the template used to store building blocks by default), and the template attached to the current document.

- **Options** This selection specifies how to insert the building block. The choices are Insert Content Only, Insert Content In Its Own Paragraph, and Insert Content In Its Own Page. The first of these choices places the building block at the cursor without adding a paragraph or page break.

➤ **To edit building block properties**

1. On the **Insert** tab, click **Quick Parts**, and then click **Building Blocks Organizer**.

2. In the **Building Blocks Organizer**, select the building block whose properties you want to edit, and then click **Edit Properties**.

3. In the **Modify Building Block** dialog box, update settings for the **Name**, **Gallery**, **Category**, **Description**, **Save In**, and **Options** properties.

4. Click **OK** in the **Modify Building Block** dialog box, confirm the operation if prompted, and then click **Close** in the **Building Blocks Organizer**.

Creating custom building blocks

You can create your own building blocks and save them to a gallery. For example, you can insert a built-in header and then use the Design tool tab to modify the header by inserting and positioning document information fields, pictures, and other elements. You can then save the header to the Header gallery, where it appears for use in other documents.

In the Create New Building Block dialog box, you define the properties for the new building block. These properties were described in detail in the previous topic, "Editing building block properties."

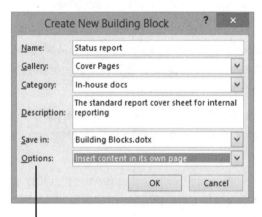

The setting in the Options list controls
how Word inserts a building block

➤ **To create a custom building block**

1. Create the document element you want to save as a custom building block. This might be a cover page, an equation, a header or footer, a table, a text box, or a simple block of text.

2. Select the element. On the **Insert** tab, expand the gallery for the type of building block you are creating, and then click **Save Selection to *Gallery Name* Gallery**.

3. In the **Create New Building Block** dialog box, name the building block.

4. In the **Gallery** and **Category** lists, specify the building block's gallery and category.

5. Enter a description for the building block.

6. In the **Save in** list, select the template in which you want to store the building block.

7. In the **Options** list, select an option for how to insert the building block, and then click **OK**.

Deleting building blocks

You delete a building block from the Building Blocks Organizer.

> **To delete a building block**

1. Expand the gallery, right-click the building block, and then click **Organize and Delete**.

2. In the **Building Blocks Organizer**, select the building block, and then click **Delete**.

3. In the message box Word displays, click **Yes** to confirm the operation.

Practice tasks

The practice file for these tasks is located in the MOSWordExpert2013\Objective4 practice file folder. Save the results of the tasks in the same folder.

- Open the *WordExpert_4-1* document, and do the following:
    - ○ Modify the header by inserting document information fields and page numbers.
    - ○ Save the header as a custom building block.
    - ○ Open the Building Blocks Organizer. Select the custom header you created and edit its properties by adding it to a custom category named *In-house building blocks*.
    - ○ Delete the custom header building block.

4.2 Create custom style sets and templates

Templates, styles, and themes all provide ways to format a Word document. Templates contain styles and define settings for page layout, headers and footers, and similar elements. Themes apply a layer of formatting that specifies fonts for body and heading text, colors for headings and other elements, and text effects such as shadows. Styles (and style sets) specify settings for fonts, paragraphs, tabs, and other formatting that are applied as a group to paragraphs and characters.

> **See Also** For more information about styles, see section 2.2, "Apply advanced styles."

This section describes how to create custom theme elements, style sets, and templates. When you work with themes, templates, and styles and style sets, keep in mind that a template is defined (in part) by the styles it contains and the attributes for those styles. After you apply styles to the content of your document, you can apply a different template or a different style set, and styles with the same name are updated to reflect the formatting defined in the new template or style set. And if the styles in a template or a document are set up to use theme fonts and theme colors, you can display a different set of fonts and colors by applying a new theme.

Themes and style sets appear on the Design tab, in the Document Formatting group, together with commands you can use to save a custom theme, save new style sets, and create custom sets of theme colors and theme fonts.

Creating custom theme elements

Themes are used in Microsoft Office programs to apply formatting to elements throughout a document. By applying a theme, you can quickly update how a document appears.

In Word, themes affect settings for colors, fonts, and text effects such as shadows. The effect of applying a theme depends on whether a document uses styles that rely on theme fonts and theme colors. If a document's styles do not rely on colors and fonts specified for themes, applying a different theme appears to have no effect.

> **Tip** Word displays theme fonts in a separate section of the Font gallery (on the Home tab) and displays theme colors together in the palettes available for fill and border colors that you can apply to shapes and other graphical objects.

When a theme is applied to a document, you can substitute a different combination of colors and a different set of fonts by selecting the preset options from the Colors and Fonts galleries on the Design tab. The Colors and Fonts galleries also provide options for creating custom configurations.

Creating custom theme colors

To create custom theme colors, you specify colors for elements such as text, backgrounds, accents, and hyperlinks. You define custom theme colors in the Create New Theme Colors dialog box. You can select a color for each element listed and refer to the Sample area to review how your selections will apply to the text and graphical elements in the document. For each element, you can select a different theme color, a standard color, or a color you mix on your own.

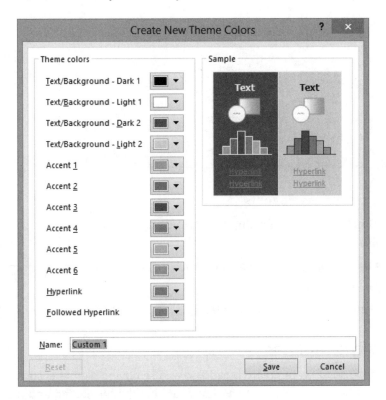

> ## To create custom theme colors

1. On the **Design** tab, in the **Document Formatting** group, click **Colors**, and then click **Customize Colors**.

2. In the **Create New Theme Colors** dialog box, display the palette for one of the elements you want to change.

3. In the palette, select a different theme color or a standard color, or click **More Colors** to open the **Color** dialog box, where you can select settings to create a custom color.

4. Repeat step 3 for each element whose color you want to change.

5. When you're done changing theme colors, enter a name for the collection of custom theme colors, and then click **Save**.

Creating custom theme fonts

A theme font is defined by a heading font and a body font. You can specify theme fonts of your own in the Create New Theme Fonts dialog box.

➤ **To create custom theme fonts**

1. On the **Design** tab, in the **Document Formatting** group, click **Fonts**, and then click **Customize Fonts**.

2. In the **Create New Theme Fonts** dialog box, select the fonts you want to use for headings and for body text.

3. Enter a name for the set of custom theme fonts, and then click **Save**.

Customizing templates

You can modify an existing template by adding and removing elements such as images, cover pages, and headers and footers and by changing the formatting and properties of styles to emphasize and organize the information the template is designed to present.

You can open a template file from the Custom Office Templates folder (in My Documents) —or from whatever folder you've used to store the template—and make changes to it as you would another document. (Templates you download from the New page or the Start screen are stored by default in your user profile, at C:\Users*user name*\AppData\ Roaming\Microsoft\Templates.) After you make these changes, attach the updated template to a new document and review the results. If you are testing the changes on an existing document, be sure to select the Automatically Update Document Styles check box in the Templates And Add-Ins dialog box. To open this dialog box, click the Developer tab and then click Document Template.

> **Tip** If the Developer tab is not displayed on the ribbon, open the Word Options dialog box, display the Customize Ribbon page, and select Developer in the Customize The Ribbon list.

Select Automatically Update Document Styles
to display changes to a template in the current document

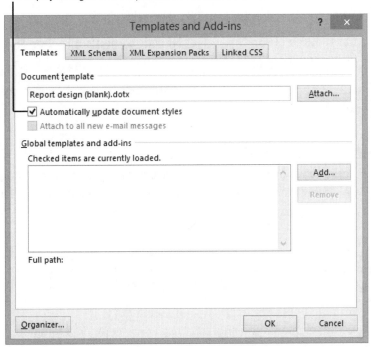

You can also modify elements of a template while you work on a document that the template is attached to. For example, you might want to distinguish more clearly the Heading 2 style from the Heading 3 style. When you adjust the style in the Modify Style dialog box, select New Documents Based On This Template. Word displays a message box when you save the document that prompts you to save the changes you made in the template.

> **See Also** For details about modifying styles, see section 2.2, "Apply advanced styles."

➤ To change a template file

1. Click the **File** tab, and then click **Open**.

2. In the **Open** dialog box, select and open the template file you want to change.

3. Make the changes to the template file.

4. Click the **File** tab, and then click **Save**.

➤ **To change a template while working on a document**

1. In the **Styles** gallery on the **Home** tab, right-click the style you want to change and then click **Modify**.

2. In the **Modify Styles** dialog box, update the style with the changes you want.

3. At the bottom of the dialog box, select **New documents based on this template**.

4. Click **OK** in the **Modify Styles** dialog box, and then save the document.

5. If a message box appears, click **Yes** to confirm that you want to save changes to the document template.

Designing your own templates

If you want to design your own template, you have a few choices as your starting point. You can use a document as the basis of the template, you can use another template file as the foundation, or you can create a template from scratch.

> **Tip** When you create a template, save the file in the Custom Office Templates folder so that the template is available when you click Custom on the New page. (This folder is created the first time you save a custom template for an Office program.)

Here are some of the elements you should consider including in a template:

- **Styles** What styles do you need? Can you work with only the built-in styles, or do you need to define each style from scratch? Depending on the purpose of the template, you need to consider styles for headings, normal paragraphs, lists, tables, illustrations and images, and other elements. When you create a style or other template feature with a color other than Automatic, be sure the color you apply is one of the theme colors, not one of the standard colors in the color palette. Theme colors will change when you change themes, but standard colors do not.

> **See Also** For more information about creating styles, see section 2.2, "Apply advanced styles."

- **Header and footer** Add page numbering, the date, a document title (for example, *Request for Proposal*), and other information (for example, the labels *Draft* or *Confidential*) that you want each document based on this template to contain in these areas. To define a header or a footer, click Header or Footer on the Insert tab and then select the format you want to use.

- **Images** Add a company logo or other graphic that should be part of each document. Click Picture on the Insert tab to add a picture to a document.

- **Page layout** Use the commands and tools on the Page Layout tab to set margins, the page orientation, page size, the number of columns, and other layout-related settings.

> **See Also** For details, see the "Using advanced layout options" topic in section 2.1, "Apply advanced formatting."

- **Document references** Add a placeholder table of contents, if applicable. If the template is for documents that include several illustrations, indicate whether captions are required and define a default style for captions.

> **See Also** For details about working with tables of contents and captions, see section 3.2, "Create and manage reference tables."

- **Placeholder text** Add placeholder text for elements such as an address block, product references, agenda items, meeting notes, and other content that should be included in documents based on the template.

- **Tables** Choose the type of table format you want. Can you use one of the built-in table styles provided by Word, or do you want to define your own?

- **Macros** Create macros that might be applicable for the template.

- **Building blocks** You can save building blocks and distribute them with templates. When you send or make the template available to others, the building blocks you saved with the template are available in the galleries.

> **See Also** For more information on creating building blocks, see section 4.1, "Create and modify building blocks."

- **Content controls** You can add certain types of content controls to a template to help you and other users manage information. For example, you can add a drop-down list control to a template, define the items in that list, and then select the items you need as you build a document. By setting properties for a content control, you can restrict the content the control allows (only certain items in a list) or provide more flexibility.

> **See Also** For details about working with content controls, see section 3.3, "Manage forms, fields, and mail merge operations."

➤ **To create a custom template**

1. Click the **File** tab, and then click **New**.

2. Create a blank document, or open an existing template to customize it.

3. Define template elements such as styles, headers and footers, images, and page layout settings.

4. Click the **File** tab, and then click **Save As**.

5. In the **Save As** dialog box, enter a name for the template.

6. In the **Save as type** list, select **Word Template (.dotx)**.

   Or

   If you included macros in the template, select **Word Macro-Enabled Template (.dotm)**.

7. Click **Save**.

Creating and managing style sets

Style sets are similar to themes in that they can change the overall appearance of a document in a single step. In addition to fonts and colors, style sets change elements such as font size, capitalization of headings, line spacing, borders, and alignment. The availability of style sets reinforces the advantages of applying defined styles to distinct document elements (headings, lists, and normal paragraphs, for example). With styles in place in a document, you can easily update the look of a document with a style set.

> **Important** Style sets change only formatting defined in styles. Any formatting applied directly to a document element is not updated by applying a style set.

A style set's definitions are contained in a .dotx file, the file name extension used for Word templates. Applying a style set does not replace the template associated with a document; it only applies the style set's style definitions.

Word stores its default style sets in the Program Files folder. For 32-bit versions of Office, the path is C:\Program Files (x86)\Microsoft Office\Office15\1033\QuickStyles. For the

64-bit version of Office, the path is C:\Program Files\Microsoft Office\Office15\1033\
QuickStyles. However, when you save a custom style set, Word prompts you to save the
file in your user profile, at C:\Users*user name*\AppData\Roaming\Microsoft\QuickStyles.

If, after applying a style set, you want to restore the formatting defined in the current
template, you can revert to using the style definitions included in that template by clicking the Reset Style Set command at the bottom of the Style Set gallery.

➤ **To create a custom style set**

1. Set up a document with the style definitions you want to use. (Start with an existing
   style set if you want to.)

2. On the **Design** tab, in the **Document Formatting** group, click **More**, and then click
   Save as a New Style Set.

3. In the **Save as a New Style Set** dialog box, name the style set, and then click **Save**.

Practice tasks

The practice file for these tasks is located in the MOSWordExpert2013\Objective4
practice file folder. Save the results of the tasks in the same folder.

- Open the *WordExpert_4-2* document, and do the following:

  ○ Apply the Savon theme to the document, and then use the Colors and
    Fonts menus to apply a different set of theme colors and theme fonts.
    Observe how the color is applied to different elements and how the
    fonts change. Add another shape to the document, and then use the
    Shape Fill command to apply a standard color. Change themes, and ob-
    serve that the color of the shape does not change.

  ○ Create a custom set of theme colors and theme fonts, and then apply
    those custom sets to the document. Use the Themes gallery to reset the
    document to the template.

  ○ Apply one or more style sets to the document and observe the changes.

  ○ Modify the Heading 1, Heading 2, Heading 3, and Normal styles to use
    different settings for font size, line spacing, indentation, and similar at-
    tributes. Save the changes as a custom style set.

4.3 Prepare a document for internationalization and accessibility

This section describes concepts and steps that help prepare a document for use by international (multilingual) readers and users with disabilities. This section's topics provide explanations of hands-on features such as the Accessibility Checker and a macro that sets the tab order in a form. This section also describes practices you can follow to help ensure that the content of a document meets general standards for internationalization and accessibility.

Configuring language options in documents

When you install Office (or Word as a stand-alone program), a single language is set up by default. The spelling and proofing tools Word provides use this language when you check the spelling of a document, for example.

For documents that contain content in multiple languages, you can add other editing languages that Word can use when it checks spelling. You set up additional languages on the Language page of the Word Options dialog box. These settings are available for any document you create in Word.

Use this list to select an additional
editing language to install

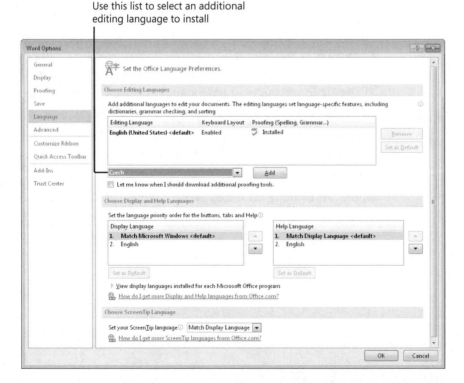

When you are working in a document, you can use the Language dialog box (which you open from the Review tab) to specify the language of selected text and then check spelling by using that language. The proofing tools for the language you select must be installed to check the spelling in that language. By default, Word prompts you if the proofing tools are missing and provides a link for downloading the tools if they are available. The editing languages available are marked at the top of the dialog box with the spelling icon.

Select text in a document, and then mark the language here to use the proofing tools for that language

➤ **To install another editing language**

1. Click the **File** tab, and then click **Options**.

2. In the **Word Options** dialog box, click **Language**.

3. On the **Language** page, in the **Choose Editing Languages** area, select the language you want to add, and then click **Add**.

4. In the list of editing languages, in the **Proofing** column, click **Not Installed**. Word opens your default browser.

5. On the **Office 2013 Language Options** page in your browser, select the language, and then click **Download** in the **Proofing tool** area.

6. Click **Run** to install the proofing tools. (This step might vary depending on the browser you use.)

7. Click **Yes** in the security dialog box, and then click **OK** to install the proofing tools.

➤ **To check spelling in a different language**

1. Select the text you want to check.

2. On the **Review** tab, click **Language**, and then click **Set Proofing Language**.

3. In the **Language** dialog box, select the language you want to use to mark the selected text.

4. Click **OK**. (You might be prompted to download the proofing tools for the language.)

5. Press **F7** to check spelling.

Adding alt text to document elements

Alt text (short for *alternative text*) is a description that you provide for an image or another type of graphical object to convey the information that the object depicts. If the image or object is not displayed or the user cannot view it (because of a visual disability, for example), the alt text you define provides a description of the information shown in the image.

To add alt text to an image, you work on the Layout And Properties page of the Format Picture pane. (The name of the pane differs depending on the type of object involved—a SmartArt object or a basic shape, for example.)

Alt text descriptions help people using a screen reader understand the content of visual objects

Use the Title field to identify the image and the Description field to provide details about the image's content. The title can be read to a user, and the user can then indicate whether to hear the full description.

> **Tip** You can add the Alt Text command to the Quick Access Toolbar to create a shortcut to the Format pane.

> ➤ **To add alt text to an image**

1. Right-click the picture, and then click **Format Picture**.
2. In the **Format Picture** pane, click **Layout and Properties**.
3. Display the **Alt Text** area, and then enter the alt text you want to use in the **Title** and **Description** fields.

> ➤ **To add alt text to a table**

1. Right-click the table, and then click **Table Properties**.
2. In the **Table Properties** dialog box, click the **Alt Text** tab.
3. Enter the alt text you want to use in the **Title** and **Description** fields.

Creating documents for use with accessibility tools

This topic describes some of the practices you can put in place to make documents more accessible to users with disabilities. It also describes how to use the Accessibility Checker to identify which elements in a document might need attention to improve the document's accessibility.

To maintain the accessibility of a document, keep the following practices in mind:

- **Add alternative text (alt text) to images and objects.** Alt text describes the content of images and other graphical objects to users who rely on a screen reader.

> **See Also** For details, see the topic "Adding alt text to document elements" earlier in this section.

- **Use headings for columns and rows in tables.** In a table, headings add context and help users navigate the table's contents.

- **Use styles.** Applying heading and paragraph styles serves not only to format a document consistently but also to define a document's structure and organization. Users working with a long document by using a screen reader rely on the occurrence of section headings to keep track of their place in a document. Keeping headings in their hierarchical order (instead of skipping a level) assists users in navigating the document and in finding information. Use the Navigation pane or Outline view to quickly view a document's heading structure.

> **See Also** For details about working with outlines, see section 2.3, "Apply advanced ordering and grouping."

- **Keep headings short.** In general, headings should be no longer than one line. Short headings aid users in navigating a document.

- **Make hyperlink text clear.** Instead of inserting a link's URL, enter display text in the Insert Hyperlink dialog box so that the destination or purpose of a link is clearly described. In addition, you can define a ScreenTip that Word displays when you point to a hyperlink.

- **Use a simple table structure.** Avoid using nested tables or merged or split cells inside a table to keep the presentation of the table's content more predictable and easier to navigate. Also avoid using blank cells in a table. Someone using a screen reader might interpret a blank cell to mean that the table contains no more data. Tab through the cells in a table to verify that the content is presented in a logical order.

> **See Also** For details about setting the tab order for form fields, see the "Using a macro to modify tab order in a form" topic later in this section.

- **Avoid using repeated blank characters.** People using screen readers might interpret extra spaces, tabs, and empty paragraphs as blanks. If a screen reader reports "blank" several times, users might assume that they have reached the end of a section or paragraph. Use paragraph formatting, indentation, and styles to insert white space in a document.

> **See Also** For more information about styles, see section 2.2, "Apply advanced styles."

- **Avoid using floating objects.** Objects that are not in line with text are more difficult to navigate and might be inaccessible to users with vision impairment. Setting text wrapping around objects to Top And Bottom or In Line With Text makes the structure of a document easier to follow for people using screen readers.

> **See Also** For more details about text wrapping options, see the "Using advanced layout options" topic of section 2.1, "Apply advanced formatting."

- **Avoid using an image as a watermark.** People with vision or cognitive disabilities might not understand an image that is used as a watermark. If you insert a watermark in a document (for example, a watermark that reads *Draft*), add the same information to another area of your document—for example, in a heading at the top of the document.

- **Include closed captions for any audio.** If you insert audio components in a document, be sure that the content is available in alternative formats, such as closed captions, transcripts, or alt text.

To check how the content of a document meets accessibility criteria such as these, you can run the Accessibility Checker. The Accessibility Checker scans a document and then displays a list of items that Word classifies in categories such as Errors and Warnings. The items listed include missing alt text for images, the infrequent use of headings, and the presence of blank characters.

Use the steps in the How To Fix area to resolve issues related to accessibility

➤ **To check the accessibility of a document**

1. Click the **File** tab.

2. On the **Info** page, click **Check for Issues**, and then click **Check Accessibility**. The **Accessibility Checker** displays the issues it detects in the document.

3. In the **Accessibility Checker**, scan the list of issues. Select an issue, and in the **Additional Information** area, read the **Why Fix** section to discover more about the accessibility issue detected, and use the steps in the **How To Fix** section to address the issues.

Managing multiple options for the +Body and +Heading fonts

In many of the built-in styles in Word, the font is specified as Body (for styles such as Normal) or as Heading (for the built-in heading styles). The fonts associated with these generic designations are set by the document's theme. If you apply a different theme that uses different Body and Heading fonts, Word changes the font to match those defined for the new theme.

You can make changes to the properties for these generic font references and to the attributes of styles that depend on them. These settings are retained when you change themes, which can apply a different set of body and heading fonts to the document's content. Some of the changes you can make can help make a document easier to understand and more accessible. For example, you can change from a colored font for headings to the Automatic setting to make text more legible to a person who is color blind.

To change properties for the styles that use Body and Heading font settings, you can work with settings on the Set Defaults page of the Manage Styles dialog box.

➤ **To specify font settings for the body and heading fonts**

1. On the **Home** tab, click the dialog box launcher in the **Styles** group.
2. At the bottom of the **Styles** pane, click **Manage Styles**.
3. In the **Manage Styles** dialog box, click the **Set Defaults** tab.
4. In the **Font** list, select **+Body** or **+Heading**, and then specify the settings for font size and font color (in addition to settings for position and spacing).
5. Click **OK**.

Implementing global content standards

When you create documents that will be read, revised, and analyzed by international audiences, you should implement standards that make the document's content easy to understand. Some of the areas you need to consider are the use of jargon and technical terms, the type of examples you provide, and the syntax of sentences.

The following list describes these and other general standards you can follow in preparing content for an international audience.

- **Use global English syntax.** Avoid long, complex sentences. Try to break down and present complicated information in tables and lists. Also, limit your use of sentence fragments, avoid idiomatic and colloquial phrases, and use the active voice as much as possible.

- **Vary references to time and dates.** Use the 24-hour time format (13:00 equals 1:00 P.M., for example). Include the time zone for event times. Instead of using numerals for months, spell out month names. Some readers will understand 03/08/14 as March 8, 2014, but others will assume it refers to August 3, 2014.

- **Use standard fonts.** Use fonts such as Times New Roman, Arial, Courier New, and Verdana, which are available in browsers and on computer operating systems throughout the world.

- **Provide a mix of examples.** If you are preparing a document that includes examples and scenarios, vary the location of the examples and the national identities of organizational and personal names and other contact information.

- **Avoid jargon.** Some terminology used in technical and professional contexts will be well understood by an audience familiar with the subject. Other times, this type of terminology will be obscure, and you should try to substitute a more familiar word or phrase. One way to help determine whether a term is jargon is to check whether the term is also used in widely read periodicals such as newspapers and magazines.

- **Strive for consistency in terminology and word choice.** Being precise and consistent in how specific terms are used aids understanding.

By selecting options for the types of issues Word checks for when it scans a document for spelling and grammatical errors, you can identify some of the issues that might make your content less understandable to a global audience. You set these options in the Grammar Settings dialog box, which you can open from the Proofing page of the Word Options dialog box. When Grammar & Style is selected in the Writing Style list, Word checks for the presence of passive sentences, sentence length, and other aspects of style that might make it more difficult for international readers to understand the document's content.

Select options in the Style list to have Word check for issues such as lengthy sentences and the passive voice

➤ **To set grammar options**

1. Click the **File** tab, and then click **Options**.

2. On the **Proofing** page of the **Word Options** dialog box, in the **When correcting spelling and grammar in Word** area, click **Settings**.

3. In the **Grammar Options** dialog box, in the **Writing style** list, select **Grammar & Style**.

4. Select the style issues you want Word to check for, and then click **OK**.

5. Click **OK** in the **Word Options** dialog box.

Using a macro to modify tab order in a form

This section describes a practical example of using a macro—in this case, a macro that sets the tab order for a series of fields in a form.

> **See Also** For more information about form fields and creating a form, see section 3.3, "Manage forms, fields, and mail merge operations."

A macro is a procedure written in the Microsoft Visual Basic for Applications programming language (also known as VBA). A procedure is a series of instructions that are saved as a unit, which can then be performed as a single instruction. In Word you can record a series of commands or keystrokes as a macro or write the macro directly in the Visual Basic Editor. You can run a macro when you need to complete the steps again later in the same document or in other documents you create.

Some of the operations you might include in a macro are:

- Applying styles.
- Changing page layout settings.
- Changing view or zoom settings.
- Entering or deleting text.
- Navigating a document.

Recording a macro and then viewing it in the Visual Basic Editor can expose a lot about what the VBA code does. (To view a macro you have recorded, click Macros in the Code group on the Developer tab in Word, select the macro in the Macros dialog box, and then click Edit.) The code in the following graphic shows three macros that select specific form fields (named Text1, Text2, and Text3).

The Visual Basic Editor provides
Project Explorer   IntelliSense to help you write code

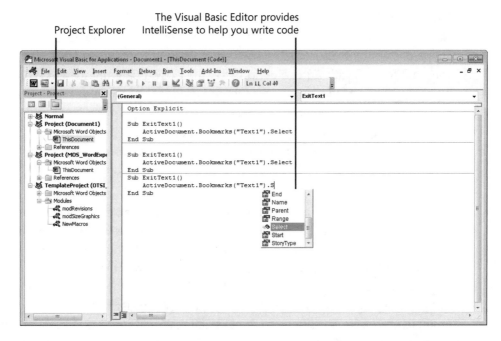

The instruction in each macro is defined within the *Sub* and *End Sub* statements. In this macro, *ActiveDocument* refers to the current document. *Bookmarks* is an object of the current document that refers to the collection of bookmarks defined in the document. The form fields are referenced by their bookmark names (enclosed in quotation marks), which are set in the Form Field Options dialog box. *Select* is a method of the *ActiveDocument* object that selects the specified field form.

The Visual Basic Editor provides tools that can help get you started working with VBA. One tool is IntelliSense, which detects the current context and displays prompts to help you write code. For example, when you enter *ActiveDocument* followed by a period, Word displays options such as *AcceptAllRevisions*, *AddToFavorites*, *ApplyTheme*,

Bookmarks, DeleteAllComments, GoTo, Save, ShowGrammaticalErrors, and many others. If you select *Bookmarks* from the list that appears for *ActiveDocument* and enter an opening parenthesis, the Visual Basic Editor prompts you to enter the name of the bookmark you want to work with. Enter a period after the closing parenthesis, and Word displays a list of methods, including the *Select* method used in this example.

> **Tip** Click Microsoft Visual Basic For Applications Help on the Visual Basic Editor's Help menu to open an extensive help system with concepts, how-to examples, and a full object reference.

In a form that includes a series of form fields set up in a table, the default tab order moves the focus across columns and then down rows. By using a set of macros such as those shown earlier, you can change this order so that the tab order moves down the fields in a column and then returns to the first field in the next column. After adding the form fields to a document, assigning bookmark names to the fields, and writing the macros, you assign a macro to each field by using the Form Field Options dialog box. In this example, the macro is assigned to the Exit action. When a user presses Tab to exit a field, the focus moves to the field specified in the Exit macro assigned to that field.

Choose the macro you want to run here

➤ **To write a Sub procedure in the Visual Basic Editor**

1. On the **Developer** tab, click **Visual Basic**.

2. In the Visual Basic Editor, on the **View** menu, click **Project Explorer**.

3. In the Project Explorer, in the **Microsoft Word Objects** area for the current document, double-click **ThisDocument**.

4. On the **Insert** menu, click **Procedure**.

5. In the **Add Procedure** dialog box, select **Sub** in the **Type** group, enter a name for the procedure, and then click **OK**.

6. Enter the code for the macro.

7. Repeat steps 4, 5, and 6 to insert additional Sub procedures.

8. Close the Visual Basic Editor.

➤ **To set up a form with macros**

1. Right-click the form field, and then click **Properties**.

2. In the **Text Form Field Options** dialog box, in the **Run macro on** area, select the macro you want to run when a user enters or exits the field, and then click **OK**.

3. On the **Developer** tab, click **Restrict Editing**.

4. In the **Restrict Editing** pane, select **Allow only this type of editing in the document**, and then select **Filling in forms** from the **Editing restrictions** list.

5. Click **Yes, Start Enforcing Protection**.

6. In the **Start Enforcing Protection** dialog box, enter a password to protect the document (optional), and then click **OK**.

➤ **To record a macro**

1. On the **Developer** tab, in the **Code** group, click **Record Macro**.

2. In the **Record Macro** dialog box, enter a name and description for the macro.

3. In the **Store macro in** list, select the template or document in which you want to save the macro.

4. Click **OK**, and then perform the steps you want to record in the macro.

5. In the **Code** group, click **Stop Recording**.

Practice tasks

The practice files for these tasks are located in the MOSWordExpert2013\
Objective4 practice file folder. Save the results of the tasks in the same folder.

- Open the *WordExpert_4-3a* document. Check the spelling of the text (in French) that the document contains.

- Open the *WordExpert_4-3b* document. Run the Accessibility Checker. As part of fixing the accessibility issues the document contains, add alt text to the images, diagram, and table.

- Open the *WordExpert_4-3c* document. Set editing restrictions to Filling In Forms. Put the cursor in the first field, press Tab, and observe the tab order. Remove the editing protection, and then write a series of exit macros so that the tab order moves down the columns instead of across the rows. The bookmark name assigned to each field is entered in the Text Form Field Options dialog box.

Objective review

Before finishing this chapter, ensure that you have mastered the following skills:

4.1   Create and modify building blocks

4.2   Create custom style sets and templates

4.3   Prepare a document for internationalization and accessibility

Index

Symbols

* (asterisk), as wildcard character, 40
@ (at sign), as wildcard character, 41
\ (backslash), as wildcard character, 41
[] (brackets), as wildcard characters, 41
{ } (curly braces)
  defining index fields, 81
  as wildcard characters, 41
! (exclamation point), as wildcard character, 41
> (greater than), as wildcard character, 40
< (less than), as wildcard character, 40
? (question mark), as wildcard character, 40

A

absolute positioning of objects, 52
accepting changes, 30
accessibility
  alt text and, 151
  checking, 154
  headings in tables and, 151
  hyperlinks and, 152
  practices, 151
  styles and, 152
  tables and, 152
  watermarks in, 153
  white space, 153
Accessibility Checker, 153
address blocks, 124, 125, 126
address lists
  connecting to external data, 121
  customizing, 122
  editing, 122, 123
  Excel workbook, building from, 120
  external data source, building from, 122
  filtering, 120, 123
  finding duplicates, 124
  managing, 121
  matching fields, 127
  Outlook contacts, building from, 121, 122
  sorting, 120, 123
  Word document, building from, 120
alt text (alternative text), 150, 151
asterisk (*), as wildcard character, 40
at sign (@), as wildcard character, 41
audio, closed captions for, 153

authorities, tables of. *See* tables of authorities
AutoCaption, 89
automark file, building index from, 79, 82
AutoRecover, 10, 11
autosaved versions, 11

B

backslash (\), as wildcard character, 41
Backstage view, 25
bibliographies, 102. *See also* source citations
Body style, font settings for, 155
book fold, 47
bookmarks
  See also hyperlinks
  creating, 73
  defining page ranges in indexes, 79, 82
  linking sections using, 74
  merge rules and, 128, 129
  navigating documents using, 73, 74
brackets ([]), as wildcard characters, 41
breaks
  column, 48
  page, 48
  section, 48, 54
  types, 53
building blocks
  categories, 137, 138
  content control for, inserting in forms, 105, 108
  creating custom, 138
  deleting, 139
  inserting, 139
  moving, 16
  naming, 137, 138
  overview, 136
  properties, 136, 137
  saving, 137, 138, 139
  ScreenTips for, 137
  templates and, 137, 145

C

capitalizing data in fields, 44
captions
  automatically inserting, 89
  closed, for audio, 153

About the author

 **John Pierce** was an editor and writer at Microsoft for 12 years. He is the author of *Microsoft Office Access 2003 Inside Track* (2004), with Paul Pardi; *MOS 2010 Study Guide for Microsoft Word Expert, Excel Expert, Access, and SharePoint Exams* (2011), with Geoff Evelyn; and *Team Collaboration: Using Microsoft Office for More Effective Teamwork* (2012), all published by Microsoft Press.

Now that you've read the book...

Tell us what you think!

Was it useful?
Did it teach you what you wanted to learn?
Was there room for improvement?

Let us know at http://aka.ms/tellpress

Your feedback goes directly to the staff at Microsoft Press,
and we read every one of your responses. Thanks in advance!

 Microsoft